# MORE THAN ENOUGH

Introduction by Larry J. Timmerman

# MORE THAN ENOUGH

Introduction by Larry J. Timmerman

B.L. Kelley

ISBN: 0-87148-619-9



Printed at Pathway Press, Cleveland, Tennessee USA

*This book is dedicated to the love of my life.*
*Her love has sustained me.*
*Her joy has infected me.*
*Her music has inspired me.*
*To her grandchildren, Josh and Austin, she is a loving tower of strength.*
*To Susan and Patrick, her children, she is the glue that holds us all together.*
*To Johnnie Wayne Rodgers, her son-in-law, he has become her son.*
*To T.L. and Ruth Forester, she is their only daughter.*
*To Jim Forester, she is his only sister.*
*To B.L. Kelley, she is a wife, a lover and his best friend.*
*Alma Ann (Forester) Kelley*
*I Love you!*
*Your Fate*

# CONTENTS

# INTRODUCTION

When you have known a person for over forty years and they ask you to write the introduction to one of their books, it is a tremendous honor. B.L. Kelley is more than a friend, he is a brother. His commitment to study God's Word has inspired me to move to another level of personal ministry. His love for God and the church is reflected in all of his writings.

**More Than Enough**, like a scintillating diamond, has many facets. The book begins with the heart-moving announcements of Christ as it related to what the disciples would face in the future. As Christ always did, He made many precious promises. Because He was God and man, he supernaturally fulfilled each one. The Spirit was the love knot binding deity and humanity into one, and the God-man known as Jesus Christ was God's only Son.

I hope you will feel the same awe as through this book, you walk from Bethlehem to the Cross, and from the Cross to the Temple area where "cloven tongues like as of fire" rested on the heads of those followers who responded to Christ's" command to wait or tarry in Jerusalem until the Holy Spirit came.

As you read this book, your desire to reach people with the Gospel of Jesus Christ will be intensified. Every minister and Christian worker will become wiser and better equipped through the Inspiration of the Holy Spirit to reach more diversified fields in the art of soul winning and building the Kingdom of God. The blood which stained the ground at the foot of the middle cross was not ordinary blood, it was **more than enough** to cover the sins of the whole world.

**More Than Enough** is a book every Christian should read. It is full of the Word of God and the message is clear. We have joy amid suffering, and affliction is a means of gladness. Our end is better than our beginning, for we are people of destiny.

Larry J. Timmerman

# PREFACE

There was always plenty of excitement around our house while growing up. I was second oldest of nine children: six boys and three girls. Leonard and Della Kelley, my parents, had their hands full with six rambunctious boys who seemed to always be in trouble. Before television, believe it or not, the supper table was a family gathering where we discussed the happenings of the day. My mother was a great storyteller, especially when relating the hardships on the farm in Alabama just west of Florence, Alabama. My grandmother, my mother's mother, died when my mother was only seven years old. Some of the hardships they endured were so thrilling the way mother would tell them, and I might add without commercial break. The title of this book comes from a comment my mother would often make at the supper table. Someone would come to the door and when they would see that we were eating would apologize, "I will come back later." My mother would yell out, "Leonard, tell them to join us. There is more than enough." "More than enough" is to say there is ample supply. When it comes to Calvary, there is ample supply of grace for every person, as well as for every sin they have committed or ever will commit. This is the promise God has given us through His death on the cross. The Holy Spirit as a comforter brings ample supply for every need you and I have or ever will have. The power that is promised through the infilling of the Holy Spirit is not short on supply. If there is a lack of spiritual power in some of our churches, it is not heaven's fault. Read the Holy Book and see the promises for yourself and then lay claim on them with the same enthusiasm that was yours when Jesus found you and delivered you from darkness into His marvelous light.

# SECTION ONE THE ANNOUNCEMENTS

Jesus made some rather startling announcements during the closing few days of his time on earth. The cross, the sin debt he was facing, loomed ahead of him like a giant boulder ready to crush him. In the Garden of Gethsemne Jesus said, "my soul is exceeding sorrowful unto death." While Jesus and his disciples were at Caesarea Philippi, he made the announcements about his ultimate goal "I will build my church and the gates of Hell shall not prevail against it." (Matthew 16:18) From that time on Jesus was on the down road headed for his destiny the cross. (Matthew 16:2) I wonder how many times he was in Jerusalem that he passed by that ugly skull barren hill and had a thought that pierced his soul, I will be back. "For this cause came I into the world." (John 18: 37; Mark 14: 34)

# CHAPTER 1

# ANNOUNCEMENTS IN THE FORM OF WARNING

Some of his announcements were in the form of warnings to alert his disciples what was ahead. He knew they would not understand it brought more questions than answers, but he also knew they would more fully understand in a few days. (John 16: 12)

**Jesus' first warning**, "Beware of the leaven of the Pharisees." (Mark 8: 15: Matthew16: 6 - 12)

The Pharisees separated themselves from everybody but people of there own kind. They were deeply religious but had developed a set of rules that nobody could follow. Jesus said, that when they made a convert they were a two folds more a son of Hell than before. (Matthew 23:15) Leaven among the Jews consisted of dough in a highly state of fermentation. Jesus was addressing their doctrine liking it to leaven when it is mixed with bread dough; it contaminates the whole loaf.

The concern of Jesus was for their spiritual health. He wanted them to be aware of being contaminated by their doctrine. The Pharisees stood out in many ways but none more evident then they're total like of mercy. There is no mercy to those who show no mercy. (Matthew 5:7)

The parable of the Good Samaritan gives us an excellent look at what is important to the religious leaders of Jesus' day. The priest and Levite deciding to walk by the wounded man fit the pattern of their lives. They did nothing unless there were people around to observe. How this parable must have stung these religious leaders when Jesus said a Samaritan, those half Jews and half Gentiles, was the one who gave aid to the wounded traveler. He took him to the inn and not only paid for his keep but also went the second mile by offering to pay if it cost more when he returned.

The Pharisees and Scribes where constantly complaining about Jesus' association with sinners and publicans. They felt that associating with these kinds of people meant he had something in common with them. This kind of attitude shows how far these religious leaders had drifted from God's plan for his leaders. It is not hard to see them pulling their self righteous robes around them and proclaiming "I thank God I am not as other men." (Luke 18: 11) Jesus gave the 15th chapter of Luke to press the point that God is concerned for lost humanity regardless of their social standing.

Listen as Jesus proclaims there is joy in heaven over one sinner that repenteth, than ninety-nine just persons, which need no repentance. (Luke 15: 7)

## The Second Warning

" My house shall be called a house of prayer for all nations but you have made it a den of thieves."(Mark 11:17)

The reputation of the house of God is to be one of prayer; it is to be noted as a place where people can pray. The houses of God where people pray where people meet God in a special way. "I will therefore that men pray every where, lifting up holy hand without wrath and doubting." (1Timothy2: 8) When we come to the house of prayer we are to lift up holy hands. This symbolic gesture of lifting one's hands represents totaled surrender a giving up to God of all our shortcomings and sins. Paul says we are to do this without wrath. Wrath carries with it the idea of smoldering resentment. The least little spark can trigger an explosive outbursts. He is saying when you come to my house of prayer don't pretend. Lift up holy hands and put away wrath.

Paul in speaking to the Thessalonians challenging them to pray without ceasing (1 Thess.5: 17), I am not sure I know how this can be accomplished what I do know is the Holy Spirit in my life is ever on guard. In a moment of time, there is an intercession to God from deep within. There is a moving, a groaning which cannot be put into words. "Likewise the Spirit also helpeth our infirmities: for we know not what we should pray for as we ought: but the Spirit itself maketh intercession for us with groaning which cannot be uttered." (Romans 8: 26) Barclay translates the last line of this verse, "with sighs too deep for words." Let me ask you, what is your church noted for; what is the reputation of your church?

Now look at the rest of the verse, "house of prayer for all nations." It is interesting that in all my years of study I have found very few comments on the word "nations" as it appears in this verse. The word "nations" means, a body of people recognized as an entity by virtue of their historical, linguistic or ethnic link. For example, look at the way Lange treats this word; "it is peculiar to Mark that everywhere lays stress upon the universality of the gospel." (Lange's commentary Mark, Page 113) Lange and many others always refer to the word "nations" in reference to the universality of the gospel. While it is true the gospel is universal it is for everybody. But this verse is talking about the house in which we worship. Jesus strongly rebuked the way the people had corrupted the temple by the merchants using it as a market place. They were treating the temple as ordinary. Jeremiah the weeping prophet declared, "Is this house, which is called by my name, become a den of robbers in our eyes? Behold even I have seen it, saith the Lord. (Jeremiah 7:11)

The corruption goes deeper than evidence by the merchants selling sacrificial doves and animals at outrageous prices to poor who come to worship. Priests took advantage of their position by taking a share of the profits and collecting an artificial, contrived temple tax from the Pilgrims and worshipers. The temple could not have been corrupted without the help of the priests. (The communicators commentary — Mark,Page 231) When one observes all the activity that surrounds the house of God today are we desecrating the house of God by some of our activity? The truth that is pressing hard on my heart is the way some people are treated because they are different. There are churches that would deny some people entrance to the house of God because they are black, Mexican or Asian or whatever is different from their particular group. One man told me, "I am not prejudiced they have their place and we have ours." Nobody should be excluded from a house of worship regardless of their social background, color of skin, lack of education or the depth of depravity. It is God's house for all people; neither you nor I have the right to stop a person who comes to the house of God. When you take it upon yourself to do so you are saying, "This is not God's house it belongs to me."

Many years ago I was scheduled to preach at one of our churches in the Midwest. I arrived early and was greeted by an old friend Joyce Albright. (Not her real name) Joyce began to relate a most interesting story. She pointed to the second row of pews where a large family was sitting. Joyce related that on their regular visitation night John informed me that he was going to a section of the city that was known for its crime and prostitution. John also informed me that he felt led to a certain house. I felt it was a terrible mistake. John would not be discouraged so I said, "where will they go to church if you do win them?" John got my message but made no reply. I can't tell you how surprised I was when he came back and had won the whole family and an another couple besides. Joyce pointed to the people setting on the second row of pews from the front to let me know that she had asked God to forgive her for her prejudice.

One pastor's wife told Alma and me wherever they pastored they reached a better class of people. This was very upsetting to us because we had led most of these people to the Lord. It appears to me that some of us need to asked God to open our eyes so we can see the harvest that lies at our own doorsteps. There is one thing for sure, you can't win what you can't see. God gives us a vision of lost humanity and let the vision include everybody. Let us repent of our preconceived ideas of what kind of people is a higher class. Let us recognize that the value of a soul is priceless even if it is wrapped in a body that seems to be repulsive. Jesus died for the whole world, no exclusions!

CHAPTER
# 2
# THE ANNOUNCEMENT IN THE FORM OF PROMISES

## The Holy Spirit of Promise

Jesus in instructing his disciples about his soon departure gave them these glorious promises "I will not leave you comfortless I will come to you." (John 14:18) While Jesus was with them he was all they needed.

However, Jesus was limited to only one place at a time. Jesus said, "... it is expedient for you that I go away..." (John 16: 7) The coming of the Holy Spirit is to be a constant companion. Jesus would not leave them exposed to the demons of Hell without a helper. "I will pray the father, and He shall give you another comforter, that he made abide with forever." (John 14: 16)

"There is no single word in our English language that can express the rich powerful meaning of Paraclete or as the king James version puts it, comforter. The word helper called out as an encourager a witness or a judge." (The communicators commentary, Roger L Fredrikson, page 232) It seems, to me we only need to look at the verses surrounding his announcement of his leaving to get a proper understanding of the Comforter's mission on earth.

## Spirit of Truth

He promised that the Holy Spirit would be a revealer of truth "Even the spirit of truth of whom the world cannot receive." (John 14: 17) The unregenerate heart has no room for truth. Jesus goes on to say to his disciples "but ye know Him." They did not understand the meaning of Jesus' statement but it had a lodging place in their minds to be brought back after Pentecost. Because he is the spirit of truth when he comes *He will teach you all things* (John 14: 26)

The Holy Spirit, the third person in the Trinity, brings a message that comes straight from God's throne. It may be a message about the last days or about some personal guidance we need for our earthly journey. Notice "He will guide you into all truth: for he shall not speak of himself. He shall glorify me: for he shall receive of mine, and will show it onto you." (John 16: 14)

The spirit will not draw attention to himself but will always point to Christ. He reveals Christ like opening up a book and revealing the contents of the book. One can only imagine the riches that are in-store for the believer who opens himself up to the Holy Spirit. The Holy Spirit can only guide those that will follow. When a person is totally self motivated, everything else comes in second. There is no room for growth in Christ and this person is a hindrance to the Holy Spirit.

The guidance of the Holy Spirit is very important to our continued growth into the likeness of Christ. John says for us to walk in the light as He is in the light. (1 John 1:7) The Psalms proclaims "Thy word is a lamp unto my feet and a light unto my path." (Psalms 119: 105) As a lamp unto my feet the word is an ever-present guide for my daily walk. As a light unto my pathway, speaks of guidance for tomorrow. It is like the headlights on my car, the low beam shines just in front of my automobile, the high beam shines farther down the road. If I want to drive to Michigan my headlights will not reach all the way to Michigan but that's not necessary. All I have to do to get from Tennessee to Michigan is to keep driving into the light and I will eventually get to Michigan. To make heaven my home, the word of God that lights my pathway does not shine all the way to Heaven. My responsibility is to keep walking in the light until heaven's gates appear. It is only reasonable to assume that if I turned from the light that the Holy Spirit reveals in the Holy Scripture, then I walk in darkness.

## The Work of the Holy Spirit in Bringing Men to Christ—John 16:8-11

Jesus promised that the Holy Spirit would be the guiding force that would bring men to Christ. "And when he is come, he will reprove the world of sin, and of righteousness, and of judgment: of sin because they believe not on me." The message is very clear it is the Holy Spirit that brings conviction. It is not our job to provide conviction through our sermons and testimonies. Our responsibility is to bear them up in prayer and be willing to stand in the gap with the Message. If we will do that the Holy Spirit will do his part. The Holy Spirit will bring to their consciousness the greatest sin of all, that of rejecting the Lord Jesus Christ.

Verse 10, "Of righteousness because I go to my father, and ye see me no more." It is the work of the Holy Spirit to bring to light the righteousness of Jesus and to unmask the unrighteousness of false teachers. Jesus has sealed the message by returning to the father and is presently sitting, and act of completion, at the father's side. He is ever there before the father making interscessiontions for us.

Before we go to the next verse I want you to notice that two-thirds of the work of the Holy Spirit, to bring men to repentance, has to do with Jesus. The one third that is left has to do with judgment. Does it not stand to reason that the greater part of our preaching should be about Jesus? The Holy Spirit left heaven's throne to represent Christ to us. The blessed Lord Jesus left earth to represent us to the father. What an unbeatable combination!

Verse 11 "of judgment because the prince of this world is judged." The prince of this world was judged and dethroned at Calvary. The judgment that the prince of darkness is living under becomes the judgment that all those that follow him will experience. While I believe that the major part of our preaching should be about Jesus, there is a warning about judgment that must not be ignored. If we will stand and proclaim the truth about Satan, the Holy Spirit will put power behind the message.

I want you to think about what I am saying. If only the Holy Spirit can bring men to Christ, and I believe this is true, then why are there so many churches that go month after month with nobody converted? I have often made the statement that nobody has ever won anybody to Jesus. The only thing we can do is to expose them to the gospel. Now having made clear the work of the Holy Spirit in bringing men to Christ I put this question to you, what more do we need to do? "He that cometh forth and weepeth, bearing precious seed, shall doubtless come again with rejoicing, bringing his sheaves with him."(Psalms 126:6) There must be brokenness and a concern that men without Christ are lost and doomed for Hell.

My life with Christ started April 1950 I was 15 years old. I remember it today as though it had just happed, I was at church that night because my Dad wanted me to go and I loved my Dad. After all these years I still remember the address of the church where I was converted 1020 Begole Street one block north of Hurley, Hospital Flint, Michigan. At the close of the service the evangelist was giving the altar call. I remember his words, "if you want to be remembered in this prayer raise your hand." I wanted to raise my hand so the preacher could see it and pray for me. But I could not get my hand up no matter how hard I tried. He then asked for all who wanted to be saved to come to the altar. I remember moving out of my seat into the aisle. I do not remember anything else. It's not that I forgot I couldn't remember that night. The last thing I remember was getting out of my seat into the aisle the next thing I remember, I raised my head from praying and there was nobody around me but my Dad and my uncle.

I shall never forget the surge of pure unadulterated joy that was flooding my whole being. It was more than I could handle, it literally was overwhelming. I have come to believe that joy is the primary evidence of conversion.

I had no idea the activity that was going on in the heavens at God's throne. I was kneeling at the altar, 1020 Begole Street, Flint, Michigan. But somewhere beyond the future star, far beyond our solar system, there is a place where God's throne abides. When my petition for forgiveness came up before the judge, Jesus stood between the judge and me and declared me to be justified based on his sacrifice and my acceptance of his death for me. When the judge declared me to be justified that allowed the Holy Spirit to baptize me into the body of Christ. (1Corinthians12: 13) When I got up from the altar I hugged my dad and my uncle. I asked how far was it home, my Dad said about 10 miles. I said let's just walk it! I felt I was only touching the ground in the high places.

## New Presence

" I will not leave you comfortless, I will come unto you." Not long into my Christian walk I became aware of a new presence with me. The Holy Spirit that brought me to Christ was the new presence. This new presence filled me with joy that was overwhelming. Peter says, "Though now ye see him not, yet believing, ye rejoice with joy unspeakable and full of glory." (1 Peter1: 8) I found that I wanted to read the Bible all the time I started reading the gospel of John, it was my favorite. The only Bible I could find was a large family Bible that was too heavy to carry. Oh how I wanted to know what it said. When I read the Bible I felt that Jesus was talking to me. He seemed to be leaping out at me from the pages. While much of what I read I did not understand, that did not stop me. I found after a while the Holy Spirit began to open up my understanding and it was like finding a gold nugget and I wanted to share it with everybody. I also found that in the first few days of my Christian walk I was indeed a new creation.

## A New Awareness

With the new presence there came a new awareness. I was more alive than ever before or at least I was more aware of everything around me. I had a strong feeling for people; I wanted to hug them all even those I previously did not care for. I felt that I needed to be careful about my words for I was conscious that Jesus was listening to me. I knew Jesus was aware of everything but before it didn't matter. There was the desire to be honest. When I was in the sixth grade I stole a candy bar and a pack of cigarettes I knew I had to make it right.

## A New Purpose

A new presence brought a new awareness that created a new purpose. I was a brand new Christian. I knew nothing about theology, I did not even know what theology was.

With the new presence of the Holy Spirit, this God given representative of Jesus my lord, I had a great desire to please Jesus. At this stage of my Christian walk I viewed God the father from the Old Testament stories. But Jesus, now that was a different story, He loved me. Now the total purpose of my life was to please Him. When something came up that I was uncomfortable doing, I would ask," would Jesus do it or would Jesus be pleased if I did it?" The whole purpose of my life was to learn as much as I could about Jesus. I had watched my Dad, who became a Christian when he was 13 years old. What a great example he was for me. This new presence in my life brought a new awareness that created a new purpose.

## The Promise of Power Unlimited

There was a time when society looked down on anybody that spoke in tongues. They were considered odd if not mentally incompetent. Now because of Christian television the average American has been brought into a Pentecostal worship service. In the last 40 years there has been an explosion of people in all walks of life and different religious backgrounds that have received the baptism of the Holy Ghost. There are hundreds of thousands of Catholics who have received this experience. All of this has been very difficult for the classic Pentecostal. We have had to learn that God is sovereign and that the Spirit moves where he pleases. (John 3:8) I have had the privilege of knowing some Catholics who were truly Spirit filled. You may not be able to explain it or even understand why God does something. But when the fruit is real, bow your head and say, "amen."

Now let us look at some of the statements John made about Jesus and the baptism of the Holy Ghost. John the Baptist seeing Jesus coming unto him declared, "behold the

Lamb of God, which taketh away the sins of the world." (John 1:29) Matthew records John the Baptist delivering a sting attack on the Pharisees and Sadducees, then he declared, "I indeed baptize with water unto repentance: but he that cometh after me is mightier than I whose shoes I am not worthy to bear; he shall baptize you with the Holy Ghost and with the fire." (Matthew 3: 11)

In Luke 24:49 and Acts 1: 8, you have similar expressions about the experience. Luke says, "tarry until you be endued (clothed) with power from on high" In Acts, Luke says, "ye shall receive power after the Holy Ghost is come upon you." The phrase "come upon you" and "endued with power" carries the idea of putting on the Holy Ghost. However, we do not put on the Holy Ghost but it is the Spirit that clothes us.

Both of these verses speak of a power that is manifested after the Holy Ghost has been received. The power is not for a platform show but for shaking the kingdom of Satan and spreading the gospel of the Lord Jesus Christ. Mark puts it a little different. "These signs shall follow them that believe; In my name they shall cast out Devils; they shall speak with new tongues; They shall take up serpents; and if they drink any deadly thing it shall not hurt them; they shall lay hands on the sick, and they shall recover." (Mark 16:17-18)

Here he puts some conditions on receiving and executing this kind of authority. It is found in the two previous verses. "Go ye into all the world and preach the gospel to every creature."

"He that believes and is baptized shall be saved; but he that believes not shall be damned." (Mark 16: 14-15) These signs will follow everyone that believes in Jesus and is willing to take this gospel or to help send it around the world.

Romans 10: 14-15 "... How shall they believe on him whom they have not heard? And how shall they hear without a preacher? And how shall they preach unless they be sent."

While all of us can't go, all of us can be a missionary by supporting those that can go and who feel that God has called them for this purpose. In John's gospel chapter 4, verses 38, "I send you to reap that whereon ye bestowed no labor; other men labor, and ye are entered into their labor." What a wonderful message from God. When you stand before the Almighty everyone who has supported a missionary will received a missionary reward.

In Saint John 7:37-39 Christ was in attendance at the feast of tabernacles the eighth day, which is the last day. In the ceremony the priest and company went to the pool of Siloam. Another priest bearing the wine of the drink offering joined the priest with a golden pitcher filled with water. They both ascended to the altar, wine and water were poured into two silver funnels leading down to the base of the altar. The people chanted, "with joy shall ye draw water out of the wells of salvation." At the pause following this ritual, Jesus stood and cried saying, "if any man thirst, let him come unto me, and drink. He that believes on me as the Scripture hath said, out of his belly shall flow rivers of living water. But this spake he of the spirit..." The prerequisite to being filled is to be thirsty. Blessed are they that hunger and thirst after righteousness for they shall be filled." (Matthew 5:6)

Out of his belly shall flow rivers of living water. The amplified says, "out of his innermost being, shall flow rivers of living water." Notice there is an "S" on river. Which speaks of many ministries flowing out to those in need.

There is the ministry of divine love.
One of the greatest needs of our world is to love people . . . Unconditionally.
There is the ministry of peace.
Blessed is the peacemaker for they shall be called the children of God Matt 5:9.
There is the ministry of comfort.
To have the desire and ability to bring comfort to hurting people.
There is the ministry of faith.
Faith sees the impossible and counts it done.
There is the ministry of divine healing.
God can and does use ministries and layman to bring divine healing.
There is the ministry of spiritual wisdom.
Wisdom is the ability to know what to do at any given time.
There is the ministry of intercession.
No ministry is more needed in the church today.
There is the ministry of helps.
To make someone burden lighter.
There is the ministry of hospitality.
Such a ministry of grace that makes even a stranger feel welcome.
There is the ministry of mercy.
Blessed are the merciful for they shall obtain mercy. Matt 5:7

One only has to look at the mighty Colorado River that has cut its path through the Grand Canyon, to realize the force and power of a river.

The Amazon River is so powerful in its flow that it pushes back the Atlantic Ocean for a distance of 50 miles. What a treat to be able to dip freshwater out of the Atlantic.

Oh God, let the mighty river of the Holy Ghost power flow to destroy the Kingdom of Satan and to establish God's kingdom. This is God's will for He taught us to pray, "Thy kingdom come thy will be done on earth as it is in Heaven." (Luke 11:2)

This mighty river of the Spirit starts its flow in Acts 2. Peter the most unlikely candidate of all the disciples, to be touched by the Spirit to preach the first message after the Spirit's arrival. He preaches Jesus with no holds barred. He put it altogether in verse 36, "... that all the house of Israel may know assuredly, that God has made this same Jesus, whom ye crucified, both Lord and Christ. Eugene Peterson put it this way, "there is no longer room for doubt God has made Him Master and Messiah this Jesus whom you kill on a cross." (The Message) "Then they that gladly received his words were baptized and the same day they were added unto them about 3000 souls."(41)

I love the next verse, "And they continued steadfastly in the apostles' doctrine and fellowship, and in breaking of bread and in prayers..." (verse 42) I like those words "and they continued. "what a mighty message for us today. There is more than enough to continue on! And chapter 5 and verse 14, "And believers were the more added to the Lord multitudes both of men and women." By chapter 6, "and the word of God increased; and the number of disciples multiplied in Jerusalem greatly; and a great company of the priests were obedient to the faith." (Verse 7)

This mighty river flowing out of your innermost being seems to gather momentum as it flows down through history. The council of Jerusalem testified as to the effectiveness of their preaching, "ye have filled Jerusalem with your doctrine." (Acts 5: 28) But the river is still flowing by chapter 17, it is said of them, "... These that have turned the world upside down has come hither also."(Verse 6) There is no stopping this river that is running throughout the land. There are those who would like to dam the river and create their own private lake. If you wanted a drink of water you would have to go to their lake. However, the message of our gospel must be "every one that thirsteth, come ye to the waters, and he that hath no money; come ye, buy and eat; yea, come buy wine and milk without money and without price." (Isaiah 55:1)

Peter who was quoting Joel, relating what God had said, "And it shall come to pass in the last day, saith God, I will pour out of my spirit upon all flesh..."(Acts 2:17) Peter further related and expounded on this promise. "For the promise is unto you and your children and to all them that are far off even as many as the Lord our God shall call." (Acts 2:39)

Is it possible that our pursuit of church growth in some cases may be more carnally motivated than kingdom related? I am not giving an excuse for empty pews. What I am saying is that in our pursuit of building a large congregation we must not lose sight of the individual. What is flowing out of the house of God is not a gimmick to get a crowd. But the whole intent is to help and minister to people. You can run your church like a star studded nightclub and you will get a crowd but there will be no Shekinah. Steve Land put it this way, some churches can appear to be like a filling station seeking only to pump blessings at a cheaper price than their competition. (Endued with power)

I am quite sure that God does not measure success as we do. God measures our success not by the size of our house, bank account or how big our church is but by our faithfulness to Him. T.L.Forester, who was pastoring one of the largest churches in Michigan, in the early fifties and sixties, was commenting to me about a man who was pastoring somewhere in the northwest. "It doesn't take a big man to pastor my church. But it takes a big man with a lot of faith and determination to pastor where this man pastores. What he was saying is, you are not successful simply because you pastor a large congregation or you have achieved a measure of success in some other field. When we stand before the Lord and he says, "We'll done thou good and faithful servant" The words *good* and *faithful* must be God's measuring rod for success.

# SECOND THE ARRIVAL

The arrival of Jesus in this world was witnessed by only a few. The heavens made the announcement with angels and a heavenly choir sang a special arranged song for this special occasion. Creation made the announcement far and wide by the showing of a special star in the heavens that guided wise men to Bethlehem to see the Baby Jesus. In contrast the arrival of the Holy Spirit was on a day when Jerusalem was filled with worshipers from all over the known world. When he arrived it was with a great sound, like a mighty rushing wind. The cloven tongues like as of fire that rested on the head of those followers who responded to Christ's command to wait in Jerusalem until the Holy Spirit's arrival.

# CHAPTER 3

# THE DAY OF PENTECOST

When the disciples were standing on the mount of Olives they were captivated by the words of Jesus. He has been with them now for forty days. During this time he would come into their presence and then disappear and they had witnessed this several times. But this was different, there seems to be a finality about his words." Preach the gospel to every creature, baptizing them in the name of the Father, and of the Son, and of the Holy Ghost: Teaching them to observe all things whatsoever I have commanded you..." He then gave one final word. Stay in Jerusalem until you are endued with power from on high. He had no sooner gotten the words out of his mouth until he began to rise off the ground. This was different than other times when he just vanished. But now a cloud engulfs him and he was gone. They kept looking into the sky looking for they knew not what. When they were shocked into reality by two men dressed in white apparel. "Why stand ye gazing into Heaven? This same Jesus who was taken up from you will return in like manner." (Acts 1:11)

## The Upper Room or the Temple?

Luke says, "they returned to Jerusalem with great joy: and were continually in the Temple praising and blessing God."(Luke 24:52-53)

Now there seems to be a conflict between tradition and what Luke says in this verse. The upper room holds a prominent place in our thinking because of what Luke says in Acts 1:13 that when the disciples returned from seeing the ascension of Jesus they went into an upper room where abode the disciples. Then in verse 14 "these all continue with one accord in prayer and supplication... the number of those gathered were about 120" (verse 15).

There is no contradiction in what Luke says in his gospel and what he writes in Acts. Look at the way the word "continually" is used in II Samuel 9:13. "So Mephibosheth dwelt in Jerusalem; he did eat continually at the King's table; and was lame on both his feet." Mephibosheth was Jonathan son and David Loved Jonathan's. King David was showing kindness unto Mephibosheth for Jonathan's sake. When the King says that Mephibosheth would eat continually at the King's table he did not mean he would never get up from the table. Whenever the table was set there would be a place for Mephibosheth. Luke is saying they were in the Temple when they were supposed to be. Acts 2:15 identifies the time of the coming of the Holy Spirit as the third hour of day, which is 9 o'clock in the morning. This coincides with the morning sacrifice and the first prayer of the day. It seems to be very clear to me the Holy Ghost fell in the Temple at the early morning prayer or at nine in the morning. It was the custom of the disciples to attend this prayer meeting. We see this in Acts 3:1, "Now Peter and John went up to gather into the Temple at the hour of prayer being the night hour."

Let me review my reasons for believing that the Temple is the place where the Holy Spirit came upon the early church.

1. The Upper Room was on the other side of Jerusalem from the Temple.

2. The crowd came to the apostle's the apostle's did not go to the crowd.

3. There is a difference between continuous and continually. The word continuous means without interruption. The word continually means when you are expected to be there.

4. No other location in Jerusalem could accommodate the kind of a crowd they had on the day of Pentecost.

5. Jesus repeatedly called the Temple "my house."

The first chapter of Acts seems to be taking care of some unfinished business. They selected one to take the place of Judas. Their method may seem strange to us but it met God's approval. Chapter two starts with the day of Pentecost. They had now been waiting for ten days. How exciting it must have been anticipating the coming of the Holy Spirit. The words of Jesus about the coming Comforter and what he would be to them must have created great expectation. The promise of power to enable them to be his witnesses beginning at Jerusalem and spreading to the end of the earth.

They arrived at the temple and were set for the early morning prayer. Whatever differences had excited between them had all been dissolved. They were all together in one place but also and more important they were in one accord. They had been praying waiting, on the edge of a miracle. When suddenly there came a sound from Heaven as of a mighty rushing wind.



CHAPTER
4

# THE WIND AND THE

The wind caught the attention, of
also the multitude that was in th
weeks. (Exodus 34: 22 Deu
Pentecost was the time for God to recei
harvest of believers to be his own speci
Bible handbook, Lawrence O Richards
was not like an ordinary wind the
horizontally; this sound was coming
wind from the North, South, East and
to in Scripture as having a purpose. Th
across the land obstructed by trees or
is in the way. However, this wind wa
straight from heaven. The wind-blow
obstructions.

This unnatural sound attracted the a
and they came running. "It filled all t
were sitting." (Verse 2) The wind ca
circle the room with a mighty intensi
whole house. Wherever the Spirit
attention. "Blessed are the people
sound." (Psalms 89: 15)

Follow the Spirit moving through
you will find there was always activi
Spirit moving, resulting in people bei

day was over three thousand souls were brought into the Kingdom of God. Fresh from their first Pentecostal infilling they were going up to pray, the time was 3 in the afternoon. It had only been a short time since the day of Pentecost. The wind that came from heaven is still blowing. As Peter and John were entering the Temple a crippled man lame from his mother's womb was waiting for some alms. I am quite sure that the two disciples had seen this man before. But this time it was different, there was a burning presence that they had not had before and what a difference it was making. Peter fastened his eyes upon him, "silver and gold I do not have, but what I do have I give you; in the name of Jesus Christ of Nazareth, rise up and walk." (Acts 3:6 NKJ)

When Peter and John were brought before the authorities, to answer regarding the healing of the lame man. I love Peter's answer, "If we this day are judged for a good deed done to this helpless man, by what means he has been made well, let it be known to you all, and to all the people of Israel that by the name of Jesus Christ of Nazareth, whom you crucified, whom God raised from the dead, by him this man stands here before you whole. This is the stone which was rejected by you builders which has become the chief cornerstone." (Acts 4: 9-11 NKJ)

This is a day of specializing and we have lots of tools to get the job done. But in reality we seem to be coming up short. We need evidence that will stand up in court. Listen to the men who wanted to put them on trial: "And seeing the man who had been healed standing with them, they could say nothing against it." (Acts 4:14 NKJ) Praise God, you can't refute that kind of evidence. If you meet a fact in the road take your hat off and bow to it only a fool will argue with a fact.

## Tongues Like Fire

After the wind, while the crowd was still gathering, a ball of fire came into the room. It was sudden, one moment it was not there and the next moment it was. It then began to separate into individual pieces appearing like cloven tongues and rested on each head. Now Israel was accustomed to the God that answers by fire. But this generation had not seen any supernatural fire, they had only heard their fathers talk about the pillar of fire that guided them out of Egypt.

## Why Tongues of Fire

The fire was a fulfillment of John the Baptist's prophecy in Matthew 3:11 "... He shall baptize you with the Holy Ghost and with fire."

The fire was a sign of God's approval in the Old Testament. When Elijah declared the God that answers by fire let him be God, shows that this was a universal acceptance of fire as a sign of God's approval.

There was a separation between the crowd and the 120 that had been waiting for 10 days. The crowd may have heard the wind but only the 120 had the fire. Then it happened! They were all (120) filled with the Holy Ghost and began to speak in tongues as the Spirit gave them the utterance. The crowd that gathered was hearing them speak in their own native tongue. Chapter 2 verse 11 tells us what they were saying it tongues. They were talking about the wonderful works of God. Paul tells us a little later that tongues are a sign to the unbeliever. (1 cor.14: 22) They were amazed that these uneducated Galileans were speaking in their own native tongue.

They were struck by something else. The 120 could not walk straight, they seemed to be drunk. "They were all amazed and were in doubt, saying one to another, what meaneth this?" (Acts 2:12)

## CHAPTER
# 5
# PETER EXPLAINS THIS STRANGE HAPPENING

Peter the anointed man of God stood up and the 11 disciples stood up with him for support and to show solidarity. These are not drunk as you suppose seeing it is only nine in the morning. The time is not right for drinking. Notice he said these are not drunk as you suppose.

You can't take new wine in old wineskins. Old wineskins are brittle and can't take the pressure of new wine. But the 120 were fresh; they had experienced the resurrection of Jesus 50 days ago and 10 days ago they had seen Jesus ascend into the heavens. For the last 10 days they had been waiting, expecting, longing, and then it happened- all heaven broke lose. The new wine from heaven was poured into these wineskins. Some standing by laughed while others poked fun, they had seen drunks before.

Peter was telling them this time it was different. The Prophet Joel prophesied what you see and hear many years ago. (Joel 2:28-32;Acts 2: 16-21) Notice how all encompassing it was "all flesh". No longer will the Jews have exclusive rights to God. Now everybody of Adam's race has the privilege of accepting Jesus as Lord and can receive the fulfillment of Joel's promise.

In the last 40 years there has been an outpouring of the Holy Ghost such as the world has not seen since the day of

Pentecost. This Pentecostal blessing that once was confined to the poor and for the most part uneducated has now invaded the hungry hearts of men and women from all walks of life.

Notice the spirit does not discriminate, "your sons and your daughters shall." There may have been a time when women were considered as second class citizens but that was never God's plan. God holds men and women of equal value to him.

Notice the young need the old, "The young men will see visions." Visions are unfulfilled realities. "Your old men will dream dreams" this means life lived, wisdom gained. Thank God you are never to old to dream

Notice no one is left out of this promise. "Servants and hand maidens." This blessing was not just for the elite, your sons and daughters, but for servants who are at the low end of the economic ladder. The rest of Joel's prophecy was Tribulation sign. The message Peter was delivering and giving the explanation of what was happening is still relevant for today.

## Peter and the First Gospel Message

In Peter's message he touches all the component parts of the gospel.

First, he establishes the lineage from David to Christ in vs. 25-30, 34,35.

Second, he establishes that Christ's life was above reproach verse 22.

Third, he establishes his vicarious suffering vs. 23, 36.

Fourth, he establishes the resurrection of Christ vs. 24, 30, 31, and 32.

Fifth he establishes his ascension verse 33.

Notice the way Peter opens his message. No diplomacy here, no back door approach. He gets their attention and then delivers a sledgehammer blow.

"Ye men of Israel hear these words; Jesus of Nazareth a man approved of God, among you by miracles and wonders and signs, which God did by him in the midst of you, as ye yourselves also know." (Acts 2: 22)

When Peter said Jesus of Nazareth they knew who he was talking about. God attested this Jesus to you through miracles, wonders and sign. Then to drive his point home says, "As ye also know." Listen very closely to what the preacher is saying. "Him, being delivered by the determinant council and fore knowledge of God..." (Acts 2: 23) All that had happened was in God's plan. As far as God was concerned Jesus was slain from the foundation of the world. (1 Peter 1:20) God was in Christ reconciling the world unto himself. You might think this would let them off the hook. However, Peter drives home the point with gut wrenching clarity "...Ye have taken, and by wicked hands have crucified and slain." (Acts 2: 23) Watch the crowd as Peter drives home the point of their guilt. How the crowd must have taken the words-you have taken and by wicked hands crucified and put to death. Whom God raised up having loosed the pains of death because it was not possible that he should be holden of it. (Acts 2:24) Notice verse 31 "... His soul was not left in hell, neither his flesh did see corruption." Peter concludes his message, "therefore let all the house of Israel no assuredly that God has made this same Jesus, whom ye have crucified, both Lord and Christ. (Acts 2:36) Now when the people heard this, they were cut to the heart and said to Peter and the other apostles, brethren what shall we do?" (Acts 2:37 NIV) Eugene Peterson says, "They were cut to the quick" (the message)

When the Holy Spirit is the power behind the message it gets results. In this day of specialization nothing can take the place of God's anointed man. I believe all heaven stands at attention when God's man stands up to preach. If the Holy Spirit was not with Peter, for this special work, they might have stoned him to death like they did Stephen. However, when the Holy Spirit is working in the minds of the unbeliever you get results. The crowd cried out "What shall we do?"

Peter was quick with an answer, verse 38 "... Repent, and be baptized every one of you in the name of Jesus Christ for the remission of sins, and he shall receive the gift of the Holy Ghost." We must not hurry through this verse. let's look at each word. He says the first thing they needed to do is to repent. We must not slide over this word and get to baptism before we know what it means to repent. Jesus said "... Except ye repent, ye shall all likewise perish." (Luke 13: 3) It is obvious what Jesus meant by the word repent. It is letting heaven know that you want God in your life.

In Luke 15: 7 Jesus says that there is joy in heaven over one sinner that repenteth. Then in verse 10"... There is joy in the presence of the angels of God over one sinner that repenteth." It is clear by the words of Jesus that to be saved one must repent. To understand this verse of Scripture you must keep it in context. The people cried out what shall we do? Peter was answering their questions-what shall we do? First you must repent, then after you have repented and God has done a work in your heart, then comes baptized. In baptism you show the world that you are identified with Christ. Look at the last line of verse 38 "... And he shall receive the gift of the Holy Ghost."

## Now Follow the Pattern.

First they were to repent, this put them in right relationship with God.

Second they were to be baptized which is a public declaration. Now stop here for second, what is their standing with God? Peter is not covering what God was doing in the heavens at God's throne. Peter was only answering their question and all of this was for or because of the remission of sins and you shall receive the gift of the Holy Ghost. "For the promise is unto you and to your children and to all them that are afar off, even as many as the Lord our God shall call." (Acts 2: 39) There is no doubt the promise he is referring to in this verse is the gift of the Holy Ghost. This gift of the Holy Ghost is for you. But not just for you but also for your children. This part of the Scripture is not difficult to understand. When he says that the promise also includes them that are afar off. Our minds go back to the words of Jesus. "Other sheep that I have which are not of this fold; them also I must bring..." (John 10: 16) You would think that we would get the message that the promise of the Holy Ghost is for everyone who follows the Lord's command in verse 38. It appears to me that he wants to take this truth beyond any possibility of misunderstanding. "As many" no set number or time "as many, As the Lord our God shall call." WHAT A PROMISE!

Is God still calling people today, is he still saying "come unto me, all ye that labor, and are heavy laden, and I will give you rest." (Matthew 11: 28) The words are wide enough to cover every form of human sin and sorrow. As a long as the sun comes up every morning and there are still people who are weary and heavy-laden, the Lord God will stand at the beginning of each day with arms outstretched saying, "COME." Just that sure this promise is for you. Joel's Prophecy will not be totally fulfilled until the rapture of the church. (1 John 3:2)

This was not the end of Peter's message with many other words he warned them: and pleaded with them, "Save yourself from this corrupt generation. Those who accepted his message were baptized and that day about three thousand were added to them." (Acts 2:40,41 NKJ)

# CHAPTER 6

# THE FIRST PENTECOSTAL CHURCH OF JERUSALEM

First, "They continued steadfastly in the apostles doctrine." (Verse 42)

This Pentecostal church had the power to continue. Jesus had instructed them to teach his followers all of his commandments. Luke opens the book of Acts with "the former treatise have I made, 0 Theophilus, of all that Jesus began both to do and teach." The apostle's doctrine that they continued steadfastly in was what Jesus taught. Clarence McClaren says, "This book tells what he continued to do and teach from the throne." A church that doesn't teach doctrine will produce weak, anemic members. A pastor can do no greater work for the kingdom of God then teach sound doctrine. There is a time when the music should stop and everybody should have a Bible along with a pad and pencil and drink in from the fountain of eternal truth.

## Second, "They Continued in Fellowship."

It is uplifting to enjoy unrestricted fellowship. One can draw from this fellowship for strength in hard times when we feel weak and vulnerable. I have witnessed in more than 40 years of ministry saints that have drawn on the strength of this fellowship when their home lives were falling apart.

When I pastored in Chicago IL. a truck driver was marvelously saved. Bill's testimony about his conversion was that Jesus got in the truck with him. Bill had been worried about dying, he was so troubled that he called his wife. It was when Bill got back in the truck that Jesus got in beside him. Bill smote his chest and cried, "Come on in, Jesus, come on in." During my time as his pastor I assigned Bill a bus to drive to pick up children for Sunday school. It did not matter what time Bill got in from the road he never missed a Sunday driving his bus. Bill's wife never attended church but this never discouraged him. He got his five children, four boys and one girl ready for church and they rode the bus with him. God honored Bill's faithfulness by calling one of his boys into the ministry. It is my understanding that he is pastoring somewhere in Kentucky. The church became Bill's extended family.

I know personally how important this fellowship is to me. There have been a few times over the past two dozen years that my world was turned upside down. If it were not for the strength of Christian friends who loved me and stood on each side of me for support, I don't know what I would have done.

It is very important to be a part of the fellowship of a local church. God is not pleased for us to be unattached to wander from one church to another looking for the best bargain blessing. When the word church is used in Scripture it most often refers to a local group of people.

## Third Continued Breaking of Bread

Not only did the first Pentecostal church of Jerusalem continue in doctrine and fellowship one feeds the mind with the truth of God the other recognizes the need for a human touch, they also came together for the purpose of celebrating the Lord's supper. Paul said, "For as often as ye eat this bread, and drink this cup, ye do shew forth the Lord's death till he come." (1Cor. 11: 26) When we approach the table of our Lord we pause in our normal pattern of worship to personally reflect on the death of our Lord Jesus Christ and on his soon return.

## Reflection on His Death

In the garden of Gethsemane Jesus' suffering was as French Arrington says "spiritual agony of bearing the sins of the world was the reality which troubled Jesus." (Christian doctrine book 2 p. 66) Jesus was plunged into darkness that lasted for three hours. Arrington says about this darkness, "This is one expression used by Jesus to describe hell" (Matthew 22: 13; 25: 30) On the cross, Jesus experiences all the fury of Hell and the spiritual agony of being excluded from the presence of the Father's light and fellowship. Experiencing the agony of a condemned soul, he cried out in despair, My God, my God, why has thou forsaken me?"(Arrington p.68) The bread represents his broken body while the juice represents his shed blood. We look back to that bleak day in human history when it was necessary for the Christ of God to be exposed physically and emotionally to the world.

But then turned your head and look toward that day when we shall see the Son of God coming with power and great glory. Don't be in a hurry to get through, let your mind reflect on the indescribable moment when we sit down around the table in heaven to enjoy with him in fulfillment of Jesus own words. "I will drink no more of the fruit of the vine until I drink it with you in my Father's kingdom." (Mark 14:25)

## Fourth They Continued in Prayer

They continued in prayer- what a formula for a healthy church. The study of doctrine, strength of fellowship, the reflection of the Lord's supper and now prayer. These four elements are the foundation stones of any local church. Prayer is more than an emergency exit when we are in trouble. There is a walk with the Lord that is an exciting adventure into the realm of the supernatural. Prayer is the lifeblood of the church. If anything happens worth while in your life or the life of the church it will be as a result of answered prayer.

## Where Are We to Pray?

Jesus said, "When you pray enter into your closet." (Matthew 6:6) When Jesus prayed he went to a mountaintop and prayed all night.

Peter prayed on top of the house. Paul and Silus prayed and sang praises in a Philippian jail. The Psalms said "evening and morning and at noon will I pray, and cry out loud: and he shall hear me." (Psalms 55:17) In I Timothy 2:8 Paul to Timothy says, "I will therefore that men pray everywhere." Where are we to pray?

In the closet or the secret place;
In the outdoors;
On the house top;
In jail;
Morning, evening and noon;
We are to pray everywhere, regardless of the situation.

## What Do We Pray for?

James says "pray for one another." (James 5:16) We are admonished to pray for those in authority. (I timothy 2:2) We are to pray for the peace of Jerusalem. (Psalms 122:6) We are told to call the elders of the church if we are sick and they will anoint with oil and pray for healing. (James 5:14)

We are to pray for our enemies and for them who despitefully use us. (Matthew 5:44)

## How Are We to Pray?

We are to pray with understanding (1 Corinthians 14: 15).
We are to pray in the Spirit (1 Corinthians 14:15).
We are to pray in one accord (Acts 2:4).
We are to pray with groaning (Romans 8:26).
We are to pray in supplication (Ephesians 6:18).

The late Dr.R.G.Lee says, "Prayer is about the only omnipotence that God has granted to humanity upon the "earth."

# THIRD THE ABIDING

The Holy Spirit came not as a special guest to abide for a little while. He came to abide forever fully ready to supply all that is needed to accomplish Christ's work in our world.

"And I will pray the Father, and He shall give you another Comforter, that He may abide with you forever." John 14:16

CHAPTER

# 7

# THE HOLY SPIRIT AND HIS WORK AS A COMFORTER

When the Holy Spirit came on the day of Pentecost he came to stay. His continued ministry among us is not due to some spiritual exuberance or some emotional excitement but based on the fact that what Jesus promised is as sure as the throne of God itself.

In the conversion experience when the Holy Spirit comes as a comforter to represent Christ there are some benefits he brings with him. We are living in a hostile environment, everything around us is pressing us to conform. The Holy Spirit as a comforter has come to help us in our journey toward heaven.

In chapter thirteen of John's gospel Jesus is beginning to deal with his disciples about his leaving and returning to his Father. This subject continues through Jesus' high priestly prayer in chapter 17. These chapters are dealing with the Holy Spirit ministry to these bewildered disciples. He will bring fullness to their live's that previously was impossible. That is why Jesus said, "It is expedient for you that I go away for if I go not away the comforter will not come, but if I go away I will send him unto you." (John 16: 7) These chapters give us insight into the mind of our Lord as he meets with his disciples for a lesson in reality before the cross.

When Jesus made the announcement about his leaving his disciples were full of question. This is not what they had been tough regarding the coming messiah and how he will accomplish his mission. Jesus gave two reasons for his leaving, first to prepare a place for them a permanent home to be with him. Second, so he could send the Holy Spirit. Jesus calls the Holy Spirit the Spirit of truth. Every ministry the Holy Spirit brings can be listed under and is an out growth of the Spirit of Truth. He is true there it is no false hood or error in him.

As the Spirit of Truth he is a teacher, his specialty is "all things." (John 14: 26) There is no subject that the Holy Spirit does know and understand. There are men and women who have made it their life's work to study the original language to delve into the difficult task of trying to understand the culture of those living in Biblical time. How I thank God for work that has been an untold blessing to so many. The vast majority of us have not had the opportunity nor the ability to pursue this kind of an in depth study. However, there is a teacher who was given on the day of Pentecost, the Holy Spirit of Truth, who knows all things and you can rest assured his information is accurate. The question I ask myself is how does the Holy Spirit teach us these truths we need to know? I have listed four possibilities. Maybe you can think of more.

First, he teaches by enlightenment. He turns the light on in your understanding. How many times have I been studying or just reading the Word of God that the Holy Spirit suddenly opens up my understanding an I was able to see truths in that passage that I had not seen before. That is the Holy Spirit teaching by enlightenment.

Second, he teaches through the anointing. In I John 2: 27, "But the anointing which ye have received of him abideth in you, and ye need not that any man teach you." When you see Peter, on the day of Pentecost, it is hard to believe this is the same man that cringed in fear a few days before. Look at him standing on both feet, utterly destitute of fear. No theological instructions could have given Peter the doctrine he preached concerning Christ's life, death and resurrection. Peter knew the things Jesus said he would know. He knew the essential relationship between Christ and God the father. He knew the mystical union of the believer with Christ. The secret is disclosed to the heart and no one sees the writing but the soul that receives it. Jesus warned his disciples saying "when they bring you into the synagogue and unto magistrates, and powers, take ye no thought how or what things ye shall answer, or what ye shall say. For the Holy Ghost shall teach you in the same hour what ye shall say."

In I John 2: 20,"Ye shall have an unction from the Holy One, and you know all things." The Unction here speaks of the Spirit, the Holy one is Christ. The meaning is very clear, God has anointed us to accomplish the task that is before us.

Third, he teaches indirectly; I mean by this that he will use people to teach us truths and many times they are not aware that God is using them. However, in Acts 18 a young man came to Ephesus by the name of Apollos, born in Alexandria, he was an eloquent speaker and mighty in the Scripture. Aquila and Priscilla heard him speak boldly in the synagogue and realized his knowledge was incomplete. "They took him unto them, and expounded unto him the way of God more perfectly." (Acts 18: 26)

## Fourth, He Teaches Through Prayer

The Spirit of Truth teaches through prayer. When one gets in the spirit of prayer there is openness to God that allows the Spirit to bring to our consciousness truths He wants us to know. I can remember a few years ago through a series of disappointments and misunderstandings that I was in need of the Lord's help. While I was praying the Lord through the Spirit communicated to me. The truth God shared with me was He cared far more about what I was than what position I held. My priorities were out of line with His perfect will for my life and that was to make me more like Him.

Paul says that sometimes we don't know how to pray. The Spirit who knows the will of God makes intercession for us with groanings, which cannot be uttered or cannot be put into intelligent speech. (Romans 8:26) This kind of praying wrought miracles in the early church and will today. The Spirit pleads the name, enthrones the name, and clains in his name, He prays in God's will, presents his promises, and decreases his power.

## The Holy Spirit as a Guide

The Holy Spirit as a teacher and as a guide are very similar, they both lead to all truth. How they arrive at their goal is different. Notice the latter part of verse thirteen of chapter 16," ... Whatsoever he shall hear that shall He speak." It is evident that he is talking about receiving his instructions from the Lord himself. "He will show you things to come." I have no doubt that he is talking about what the disciples will face in the days just ahead. But it also has a meaning for us today. With the emphasis on "all truth" gives special meaning to Jesus' words, "He will show you thing to come." I believe that God cares about everything that affects his people and will, when necessary give guidance.

The next verse gives the continuous of his guidance the Holy Spirit will glorify Christ. The Holy Spirit is especially suited to reveal Christ to us because he knew him before the beginning of time. He shall glorify me: for he shall receive of mine and show it unto you." (16: 14) What does he mean by the word glorify? To glorify means to give honor to magnify, to praise, to worship. When the Holy Spirit begins to unveil Christ in all of his glory to a human soul you come away feeling the half has not been told me. The depth of Christ is unsearchable. The love of Christ is beyond human understanding. The grace of Christ is immeasurable, the glory of Christ is unfathomable, the mercy of God is unbelievable.

The comforter as the spirit of truth will testify of Christ (John 15: 26). To testify is to be a witness, to give evidence regarding the reality of the Lordship of Christ. In reading the book of Acts you can see how the Holy Spirit used godly men in the most difficult situations to give evidence of their faith in Christ. I am thinking of Peter whose cowardly act of denial was washed away by a flood of Holy Ghost power. Standing before some of the same men who condemned Christ to death said, "but ye denied the Holy One and the Just, and desired a murderer to be granted unto you; and killed the Prince of Life, whom God had raised from the dead; whereof we are witnesses." (Acts 3: 14-15)

I am thinking of Stephen whose testimony caused the angry mob to hurld stones at his exposed body. While they witness his angelic face God got a hook in the jaw of one by the name of Saul, who after he was saved shocked the Roman Empire and many of Caesars' household became Christians. Saul, who latter became Paul was arrested by Christ and went from being Barnabas' assistant to become one of the most powerful voices for Christ in all of the Gentile world.

The Holy Spirit is still testifying today for Christ through godly men and women. I am thinking of Bill and Lorraine Alton whose lives were spent in the foreign service for Christ. After years of missionary service they decided to retire. The church gave them a retirement celebration and they were expected to spend the rest of their lives in leisure. However, after a few months found Bill and Lorraine headed for Mexico because one of our schools needed their expertise. Then there was Margaret Gaines whose selfless life for Christ among the school children in the small village of Aboud has become a living memorial to Christ.

" When he is come he will reprove the world of sin, and of righteousness and of judgment." (John 16:8)

This verse shows a different purpose for the Holy Spirit than what we have learned so far. The other ministries have to do with the followers of Christ. This one has to do with those who are out of the ark of safety. The work of convincing men and women of their sins and their need of a savior is the work of the Holy Spirit. We are mere messengers, only channels, for the Lord to work.

There is a spiritual law that is not written but implied that God will do nothing except in answer to prayer. Jesus said, "Lift up your eyes and look on the field for they are already ripe onto hearts." (John 4:35)

"Pray ye that the Lord of the harvest that he will send forth laborers into his harvest." (Matthew 9:38) God responds and sends workers for the harvest when we are sincere and ask for them. I wonder if is not offensive to the Lord that so much of our prayer time is done while we are doing something else. While I know we are all busy is it not a lack of respect for the Lord of Glory that we are unable to give him a few minutes of uninterrupted time each day.

A few years ago I was living in Maryland, just outside of Washington D. C. one day a friend who worked at the Capitol police force, asked if I would be interested in getting a close up view of the President of the United States. I said yes. Very excited I dropped everything I was doing, nothing was more important to me than seeing the president. What does that say about the casual way we come into the Lord's presence?

When the Holy Spirit is prompting us to pray and we ignore the prompting something the Lord wants to do is not accomplished. When our worship services are run like a track meet we can't wait to get it over with so we can do something we really enjoy. I have felt at times that some people feel their church attendance is a sentence handed down by the great judge in the sky so they can win his favor and can go to heaven when they die. When these conditions exist there will be no conversion of sinners and heaven will have no reason to rejoice.

Let us open our hearts to him and pray, "Come Holy Spirit, use us for your glory. Help us to be an uninterrupted channel for the Lord to do his work. Lord help me not to be a hindrance to the Holy Spirit in his pursuit of souls.

CHAPTER

# 8

# THE FULLNESS OF THE SPIRIT

The work of the Holy Spirit as a comforter and the benefits he brings with him are well documented. "For by one spirit are we all baptized into one body..." (1 Cor.12: 13) The Holy Spirit is the agency that brings us into the body of Christ. However, there is an experience with the Holy Spirit that is for those who already belong to Christ. In Matthew 3: 11 John the Baptist speaking of Christ said, "... He shall baptize you with the Holy Ghost and fire." In the conversion experience the Spirit does the baptizing into the body of Christ. In what John calls the baptism of the Holy Ghost, Christ does the baptizing into the Holy Spirit.

And Luke 24: 49, "Behold I send the promise of my father upon you." This is a gift from heaven a gift that speaks of a relationship. "But Tarry ye in the city of Jerusalem until ye be endured with power from on high." The ASV uses the word "clothed. "Tarry until ye be clothed with power. The TCNT uses the word "invested." Tarry until ye be invested with power. The NEB uses the word "armed." tarry until ye are armed with power. This kind of tremendous power that is promised to all believers is for a special purpose. The reason is preceded by the promise, Luke 24: 47-48.

"And that repentance and remission of sins shall be preached in his name to all nations, beginning at Jerusalem. And ye are witnesses of these things."

Here the Holy Ghost is connected with preaching and the ingathering of souls for the ultimate purpose of building his church.

There was more that happened on the day of Pentecost than just the Holy Spirit coming as a comforter. They were being invested with power to accomplish the great work of bringing Jesus to the nations.

Acts 1:8 gives the same basic promise and responsibility that is given in Luke 24 "ye shall we receive power after the Holy Ghost is come upon you." How is this power manifested in one's life? By producing an inner confidence that creates boldness. When his power is manifested he will give you a word that will fit the accession. There will be an ability to operate in the natural with a confidence of guidance. This wonderful anointing will cause the singer to sing better. He will cause the preacher to preach with greater clarity. The Holy Spirit will take the message to the heart of the one in need with a penetrating force that creates expectance. He will make the great commission possible. There is an awareness of God's presence that he is working now. "... And ye shall be witnesses unto me."

I understand that at that time there was no word for witness. They use the word "martyr" to describe anyone who was totally committed to his faith. What Luke was describing in Acts 1:8 was not just a simple testimony but a dedication, a life style, a total commitment.

Paul by Divine revelation has given us a glimpse into the supernatural world of spiritual wickedness. "We wrestle not against flesh and blood but against ... spiritual wickedness in high places." (Ephesians 6:12) The supernatural battle we face cannot be won with natural talent, it is a spiritual battle. Only through the power we received through the Holy Ghost are we able to fight in the supernatural world. I feel that some of the same battles we face on the mission field with demon forces we are facing in the U.S.A. Our nation has given itself over to wickedness that is eating at the heart of our religious freedom. This wickedness would like to put all Christians under house arrest. At this hour when the forces for the anti-Christ are drawing closer it is not going to be business has usual. These are desperate times and it demand we lay all on the line for Christ.

Let me encourage you, at this moment, to lay down this book and ask God to fill you with his power. Be open to him, let happen whatever he wants to happen. Don't be afraid!

The purpose of the Holy Spirit is not only to help us in our journey toward heaven, but also to equip us with power to exercise the authority Christ has given us. If evil spirits will wax worse and worse, deceived and being deceived; if in the last days it will be perilous times,(perilous-meaning dangerous times,) with this truth in mind it is apparent that we need this supernatural power today as much as they needed it in the early church.

It is time the church became desperate. The late Vance Havner used to say, "The problem with the church is the world is desperate but the church is not." The wise man in proverbs, "... He that sleepless in harvest is a son that causes shame." (Proverbs 10: 5) In Luke 24: 47 he uses the word nation, "... Repentance and remission of sins shall be preached in his name to all nations beginning at Jerusalem." And Acts 1: 8, "...Ye shall be witnesses unto me in Jerusalem and in all Judea and Samaria and unto the utter most parts of the earth." The divine plan of God is for the church to carry his gospel around the world nobody, no village, no metropolitan city, is to be left out. That's God's plan you are either implementing it, or hindering it, no one is neutral!

# FOURTH THE ABILITY

When I use the word ability, I am thinking of skill, resource and sufficient power. When I add the Holy Spirit to the word ability, I think of Eph. 3:20, "Now unto Him that is able to do exceeding abundantly above all you ask or think, according to the power that worketh in us."

# CHAPTER 9

# ACTS AS A BLUE PRINT

When we look for a pattern, a blueprint, in building the local church what has God given us as an example to go by? There is no doubt that the Epistles are helpful but most of them were written to correct problems that existed in an already established church. Only the book of Acts gives us a look at the church in its embryonic stage. Why did God allow the book called Acts of the Apostles to be included in his holy book if it were not intended to be used as a guide? It has only been recently that the book of Acts was looked upon as not being suitable for doctrine because it is only history. Luke in writing this book, under the guidance of the Holy Spirit, was not strictly speaking, writing a history of the early church. The task of a historian is to give a comprehensive narrative of all of the important facts. Nothing is said about the church in Galilee, the evangelizing of Egypt and Rome. No explanation on how James came to a place of leadership in the Jerusalem church. No explanation of what Paul did in Tarsus after his conversion. Luke is telling a story, not writing a history. (Wycliff Bible Commentary, Acts, pg. 381)

Lloyd J. Ogilvie gives a good account of the purpose of this book.

"Acts gives a biography of the Holy Spirit. The risen Christ, from the time immediately following the resurrection through the birth and growth of the church. It is not a historic account of a one time, never to be repeated affluence of the Spirit, but a stirring benchmark the irreducible maximum for Christianity in any age. (The Communicator Commentary, Acts, pg. 15)

It seems to me that Acts is a teacher of the struggles and victories of the early pioneers of the new church age. The Holy Spirit filling them with power to challenge their generation with the message of Jesus Christ, the crucified but risen Lord.

Ogilvie further states, "What happened then can and is happening today. Acts cannot be studied without the honest question why is that power, vitality, excitement and joy so seldom evident in our lives and church today? (PG.15)

This is a very penetrating question. Let me give you one more quote from Ogilvie as in minds eye he climbs to the highest mountain and declares, "the unquestioned conviction that we are living in the most exciting days since Pentecost in which the book of Acts is both are charter and our challenge." (pg.15)

When we read the book of Acts we are not reading about some bygone days of yesterday but a guide, a blue print to show us what God intended for the church in the here and now. I know from experience that when you are building a house you have the blue prints on the job so you can, at times, look them over to see if what you are building corresponds to the blue print. If it is not you make whatever adjustments are needed. It appears to me that it is time we took inventory. Let all the saints gather in the church, naile a sign to the front door that says closed for inventory.

There are some Christians that want to dismiss tongues as the primary evidence of the Spirit Baptism. They say that the book of Acts cannot be used to establish doctrine because it is basically historical. I have already laid the groundwork to dismiss this objection by quoting men who are not Pentecost. Let me ask you a question. How is doctrine established? Paul says, "All scripture is given by inspiration of God and is profitable for doctrine." (2 Tim. 3: 16) That ought to settle the question on what is used to establish doctrine. If what you and I believe is not fully established by the word of God it will not profit us in our pursuit of God.

To read the Acts of the Apostles you cannot help but notice how God dealt with them about what was important to him. It seems to me that doctrine is what God does in a consistent manner over a period of time in dealing with mankind that is documented and established by the word of God. If this is a sound definition of how doctrine is established then we have excellent evidence to believe that speaking in tongues as the Spirit gives the utterance is the primary evidence of the initial infilling of the Holy Spirit.

F. J. May in the introduction of his book on Acts says, "It is a book of great preaching revealing the basic theology of the early church." "This book is a witness of apostolic doctrine and primitive Christianity; a rule and a guide for government. The discipline and the order of the church; and armor which furnishes the church with weapons in its conflict with Antichrist; a repository that offers a remedy for every soul-destroying disease engendered by error in faith. A storehouse which abundantly nourishes faith, patience and hope. A mirror and stimulus promoting love and her appropriate works. A treasurer bounding in learning and sound doctrine." (Lange's Commentary, Volume 9, pg. 2 Acts)

There are four incidents where people received the initial infilling of the Holy Spirit that speaking in tongues takes place at the time of the infilling.

1) In Acts 2:4, "And they were all filled with the Holy Ghost, and began to speak with tongues as the spirit gave them utterance."

2) In Acts 10: 44-46, "while Peter yet spake these words the Holy Ghost fell on all them which heard the word. And they of the circumcision which believed were astonished, as many as came with Peter, because that on the Gentiles also was poured out the gift of the Holy Ghost. For they heard them speak with tongues and magnify God..."

In both of these passages the speaking in tongues occurred at the time of the infilling. In the second passage it occurred some 8 to 10 years after Pentecost. "While Peter was speaking the Holy Ghost fell on all of them which heard the word." (Acts 10: 44)

I have been in a worship service where the Holy Ghost fell upon the people and the sovereign God reigned supreme and mighty things happened. The word "fell upon" means simply that the Spirit gripped them, he took possession of them. Later Peter had to explain his conduct to the leaders of the church in Jerusalem. They wanted to hear from him why he had broken the social barrier with the Gentiles by eating with them (Acts 11:3).

Peter defending himself gives a straightforward answer of his experience.

"And as I began to speak the Holy Spirit fell upon them, as upon us in the beginning. Then I remembered the word of the Lord, how that he said, John indeed baptized in water; but you shall be baptized with the Holy Spirit. If therefore, God gave them the same gift as he gave us when we believed on the Lord Jesus Christ, who was I that I could withstand God? (Acts 11:15-17)

3) In Acts 19, some 20 years after Pentecost, Paul arrived back in Ephesus to find 12 disciples who knew only the baptism of John. Paul asked them a very direct question, "... Have you received the Holy Ghost since ye believed?" (Acts 19: 2) John Rea in his book, Bible Handbook on the Holy Spirit says, "Having believed, is the same as in Ephesians 1:13.There the context clearly brings out the fact that the gift of the Holy Spirit comes to us as a consequence of our believing in Christ." In verse 6, "and when Paul laid his hands upon them, the Holy Ghost came on them and they spoke with tongues, and prophesied."

With the three incidents I have related we can arrive at some conclusions. First, in every case tongues was the primary evidence that occurred at the time of the infilling. Second there were other evidences that followed, tongues was only the first.

In chapter 8 the revival in Samaria speaking in tongues upon receiving the gift of the Holy Ghost is not so evident. However, many Bible commentaries believe that what Simon the sorcerer saw and observed was speaking in tongues by the new converts at Samaria.

F. F. Bruce, The Book of Acts, pg. 81 "The context leaves us in no doubt that their reception of the Spirit was attended by external manifestation such as had marked his discent on the early disciples at Pentecost."

Here you have four incidents where speaking in tongues are directly connected to receiving the gift of the Holy Spirit from the hands of Christ. Let us look at one more biblical example in Acts 9. Here the Lord Jesus Christ had arrested Saul, while on his journey to Damascus. Soul the persecutor of the saints has received a personal visit from Jesus himself.

Saul was so affected by this visitation that Luke says, "He trembling and astonished said, Lord what will thou have me do? And the Lord said unto him, arise and go into the city, and it shall be told thee what thou must do." (Acts 9:6)

God tapped one of his special servants by the name of Ananias, not a preacher or an apostle just one of Jesus followers, who arose for this special assignment and we never read of him again. When Ananias came to Saul with the message from the Lord and to lay his hands on him to receive his sight and be filled with the Holy Ghost there is no mention of speaking in tongues. However, in the Corinthian epistle Paul says, "I speak in tongues more than ye all." (1 Corinthians 14:18) Notice Paul does not say I spoke in tongues but I speak in tongues, it was a continuous experience. In keeping with the other places where the infilling of the Spirit took place it is reasonable to assume that Paul spoke in tongues at the time he received.

Moses gave the standard by which judgment is to be made. A murderer could not be put to death on the testimony of only 1, there had to be 2 or 3 witnesses. (Deuteronomy 17: 6) Murder was to be avenged by the community. In the New Testament Jesus gave instructions on solving problems in the community of believers. It is to be done with two or three witnesses. (Matt.18: 16) Paul in II Corinthian's 13: 1 writes, "This is the third time I am coming to you. In the mouth of two or three witnesses shall every word be established." The responsibility to provide two or three witnesses was established in the law by Moses. Jesus recognized it and Paul adopted in his dealing with churches he established. Paul says every word is to be established by two or three witnesses. It seems to me that God in dealing with such gross sin by the witness of two or three persons (and that is sufficient to put a man to death) then this must be God's methods of establishing what is important.

In establishing tongues as the primary evidence of the baptism of the Holy Ghost we have four reliable and undeniable witnesses that say speaking in tongues will happen when one is baptized in the Holy Ghost. The Scriptures that pertain to Paul receiving the Holy Ghost and speaking in tongues is circumstantial. If you discount Paul's baptism then you still have a problem, for that would mean that 80 percent of the time people receiving the Holy Ghost would speak in tongues as the Spirit gave them the utterance. According to the Scriptures that I have quoted pertaining to the establishment of a word, (doctrine) all that is needed is 2 or 3 witnesses and I have more than met that standard with four incidents.

There are seven times when the words full or filled with the Holy Ghost where speaking in tongues is not mentioned. There are times even though a man maybe full of the Holy Ghost, there is a need for an excess of power for a specific purpose. In chapter 3 the lame man was healed and it caused quite a stir among the people. Peter and John found themselves in trouble with the rulers and elders of Israel. Caiaphas the High Priest and other notables were gathered in Jerusalem. They sat in a circle putting the two apostles in their midst. The question they posed to them, "By what power or by what name have ye done this." (4:7)

"Then Peter filled with the Holy Ghost, said unto them, ye rulers of the people and elders of Israel" (V.8) Peter who had already been baptized with the Holy Ghost on the day of Pentecost is filled again; filled for a special objective. Filling of the Spirit in terms of power to perform a given task.

In Acts 4: 5-6, Luke began by naming those who were present. "And it came to pass on the morrow, that the rulers, and elders, and scribes, and Annas the high priest, and Caiaphas, and John, (this is not John the Apostle) and Alexander, and as many as were of the kindred of the high priest, were gathered together at Jerusalem." Peter delivered a stinging answer to their question. "If we this day be examined of the good deed done to this impotent man, by what means he is made whole. Be it known unto you and to all the people of Israel, that by the name of Jesus Christ of Nazareth whom ye crucified, whom God raised from the dead, this man stands here before you whole." (V. 9-10) After spending a night in jail the rulers wanted to punish them more. But they found it impossible because the man who was healed was standing in their midst. They threatened them and warned them not to preach anymore in the name of Jesus. Peter and John when directly to their own people and told them all that the chief priests and elders had said to them. They had a prayer meeting not to complain to God about their treatment. They prayed for God to heal and that signs and wonders may be done by the name of the holy child Jesus. Then in verse 31 "and when they had prayed the place was shaken where they were assembled together; and they were filled with the Holy Ghost and they spoke the word of God with boldness."

There is something awesome about the Holy Ghost moving with such force and power that we are transformed into a blazing torch for the Resurrection. This can and should happen today and if it did, people would find it more difficult to resist his presence. They may say of us like they did of Peter and John, these men are ignorant and unlearned men. However, let them also recognize that we have been with Jesus.

to avoid ultimate judgment is very simple, abide in the vine. Let grace teach us how to keep the life of Christ flowing into and through us.

John also uses the word love to unfold to us the same message. He bridges the gap with verse 11, "These things have I spoken unto you, that my joy might remain in you and that your joy might be full." Then Jesus gives us this great command, "... That ye love one another as I have loved you." (12) The way the world knows we belong to Jesus Christ is if we have love one for another. (John 13:35) This is a very strong and direct statement from our Lord regarding our conduct towards our fellow traveler in this journey of life. No man can claim forgiveness for his own sins and neglect his debt toward others.

There is a moving statement in verse 9 of chapter 15, "as the father has loved me." Now that statement says a lot about love and suffering. We often say, "God, if you love me why am I going through such pain?" Notice the whole verse, "as the Father has loved me, so have I loved you: continue ye in my love." One translation puts it this way, "I have loved you just as the father has loved me. You must remain in my love." (Charles B. Williams) This says that sometimes God has a higher priority than just to keep us from suffering or to make us comfortable. This verse is also very clear while God holds on to me, I have to use my God given will power to remain in his love. Let us offer this prayer, "Lord have your way in my life and whatever the circumstances let my life show forth your glory in Jesus' name. amen." The apostles felt it was an honor to suffer for their Lord. I don't advocate the persecution of the saints but I tell you the truth it would separate the confessors from the possessors.

Let us look at the way prayer is used in these three chapters. In John 14: 12-14 are some of the most exciting statements Jesus makes to the disciples and to his posterity. "... The works that I do shall ye do also..." In order to get an understanding of the works Jesus did we must look at Luke 4:18-19. Here he lists what he was sent to do in his earthly ministry. Preach the gospel, heal the brokenhearted, proclaim liberty to the captive, recovering of sight to the blind, set at liberty those that are oppressed, proclaim the acceptable year of the Lord. The church through anointed men and women has seen all of these works in our midst. However, he goes one step further when he adds, "and greater works than these shall ye do also because I go to my Father." There is no doubt that he is talking about the coming of the Holy Spirit that will not be confined to a single human body or to a specific location. There is no limit to his presence and power. However you interpret the words "greater works," it is a fantastic promise. The next verse says, "and whatsoever you ask in my name, that I will do, that the Father may be glorified in the son." (Verse 13)

The key to understanding, I feel, is in the last line. "... That the father may be glorified in the son." It appears to me that he is talking about the harvest of souls. God was in Christ reconciling the world unto himself. If the term-greater works-is talking about greater in scope rather than greater in-kind, then we have seen the fulfillment of this promise in the last few years. If this is the case, then verse 13 and 14 have a direct link to the greater scope of spreading the gospel.

We have been looking at our responsibility to abide in the vine. Take one more look at verse 6. "If anyone does not abide in me he is cast out as a branch and is withered and they gather them and throw them into the fire, and they are burned." Now I want you to notice the branch does not wither until it is cast out or as another verse puts it, cut off. There is a time in which the diseased branch still looks like all of the others but there is death working in its system. One can have all the externals right and appear very spiritual but internally the life of Christ is being hindered. We have a responsibility to abide in the vine. How many times after hearing what some friend has done that was immoral, I have commented "that is not like him how could this happen?" The truth lies somewhere in my friends past. There arose a hindrance in the life of my friend that causes the life of Christ to take second place. It never starts big but it grows fast and before long you are trapped. The branch was severed from the vine. There is a time when the analogy of vine and the branch no longer works. There is praise be unto God the miracle of restoration.

CHAPTER

# 11

# THE SPIRIT CONTROLLED LIFE

## The Problem With the Flesh

You can ask a hundred people what does it mean to walk after the flesh. You will get a quick answer with illustrations. But ask the same people what it means to walk in the Spirit and they will stammer or say very little or will feed you something so complicated and unreasonable that no one could understand must less achieve. We are more acquainted with what the flesh gives us than we are at what the Spirit brings us. Walking in the Spirit carries with it the idea of living every day with a conscious awareness of the spirit's guidance. It is something that happens on a day by day basis. It is not a once and for all experience. Every day when you roll out of bed the flesh will be waiting for you.

We know the fruit of walking in the Spirit. They are found in Galatians 5:22, 23 This seems to be the only internal defense against fulfilling the lust of the flesh. Paul says, "... walk in the Spirit and you shall not fulfill the lust of the flesh." (Galatians 5: 16 K J) We know that the flesh and the spirit are pulling from different directions. The reason we know more about the flesh is because we have been acquainted with that side of our life before we got out of the baby bed. At every turn of the road we have learned about the big "I". I come first. We start out in this world with our fleshly desires crying for attention from the baby who has learned that if he cries long and loud enough he will get whatever he wants. That's not a lot different than an adult who has lost all semblance of discipline and will do anything to get his own way.

The whole idea is self is dominant, self is king. You have listed in Galatians 5: 19-21 all the fruits of this kind of living. You go from sexual immorality to orgies, all that is between is a sorry company to live with. We must realize that the flesh and its lust is our enemy and must not be treated as a controlled friend. And enemy is one whose ultimate goal is to devour you. There are some legitimate needs of the body that are necessary for good health. The body is not our enemy, it is only a servant, it will obey its master. Paul says in Philippians 2:5, "Let this mind be in you which was also in Christ Jesus." The NIV put it this way, "your attitude should be the same as that of Jesus Christ." Your attitude determines what is important to you

John wrote under the inspiration of the Holy Spirit, "Love not the world neither the things in the world. If a man love the world the love of the Father is not in him." (1 John 2: 15 —17) He goes on to tell us what he means by the world. First, is the lust of the flesh, which is the pulling of our fallen nature.

Second, is the lust of the eye. The eyes are the gateway to the soul and feed the lust of the flesh. It is important that we make a pack with the Lord, "I will not allow my eyes to contaminate my soul." "All the ways of a man are cleane in his own eyes..." (Proverbs 16: 2) Solomon was an observer of life and he came to the conclusion, "Hell and destruction are never full; so the eyes of man are never satisfied." (Proverbs 27: 20) We keep reaching for something more, we feel if we can only get that - whatever that is-then we will be happy and satisfied. However, we soon learn the dream is elusive and it did not bring the fulfillment we had hoped for.

The flesh has an insatiable appetite for more. This generation has tried to legitimize the unholy and has presented it as normal. "There is a generation that are pure in their own eyes and yet is not washed from filthiness." (Proverbs 30: 12)

Third, in this list is the pride of life. Prides well have its way regardless of the consequence. This kind of pride is idolatry, it is the worship of self. The Apostle John says that if you love the world you don't love God.

Notice if you will, the stumbling block for most of us is found in the same verse as love not the world. We have been very clear about what the Bible means by the lust of the flesh and eyes and the pride of life. But notice these words, "neither the things in the world." (V.15) There is a drive to accumulate things, not evil things, just things. The U.S.A. accumulated credit card debt is unbelievable at the end of the year. Far too many of us have become slaves to things. We are told not to love the things of the world. Love is a very strong word it goes beyond the mer fascination to mean the controlling interest of your life. Do you get the subtle approach of Satan to keep you from doing the will of God? We may castigate someone whom we feel is to worldly and yet be consumed with the accumulation of things. It is not wrong to want to better yourself and to have a nice home and other amenities of life. The sin comes in when we allow that to control our life when it becomes such an obsession that it literally becomes our security blanket. Jesus told about a farmer in Luke 12:16-20 that was so successful that he decided, "...This will I do: I will pull down my barns, and build greater; and there will I bestow all my fruits and my goods. And I will say to my soul, soul, thou has many goods laid up for many years; take thine ease, eat, drink, and be merry. But God said unto him, thou fool, this night thy soul shall be required of thee: then whose shall those things be, which thou has provided?"

Paul says, that all those in Christ Jesus are a brand new creation. (II Cor. 5:17) This means that the child of God has a new desire in his heart and that has changed his outlook on life. When you leave the place of conversion you soon find out the battle is not over it has only just begun. The flesh will say, "Let's have some fun." The new created spirit will say, "No we don't do that anymore." The flesh replies "What do you mean? Ever since we have been together we have done what I wanted." But the Spirit says, "we are now under new ownership." The Bible calls it crucifixion or sanctification. "They that are Christ's have crucified the flesh with its affections and lust". (Galatians 5: 24) Again Paul says, "... Count yourself dead to sin but alive to God in Jesus Christ." (Romans 6:11 NIV)

Jesus said that love is the true mark of identification. When love is expressed toward God you keep his commandments. When love is expressed toward people, especially those of the household of faith, the world knows you belong to Jesus.

Let me give you truths that will help you to walk in the Spirit. Our objective is to know how to live in the Spirit. If we learned that well enough we won't have to worry about the flesh. (Galatians 5:16)

## Living in the Spirit Is Walking in the Light of God's Word.

When we live and walk in the Spirit there will be obedience to God's word. There is a lot of miss information based upon the prejudice of the teacher. However, everybody must answer for themselves on what the Bible teaches. I have made my beliefs in the Baptism of the Holy Ghost known in a previous chapter. You have a responsibility to search the scripture and to either accept or reject. We have the privilege of walking in the light as he is in the light. We then have fellowship and cleansing. (1 John 1:7) Walking in the light denotes progress, the light of Jesus reveals truths that we must obey to remain in the light. You must not ignore the fullness of the Spirit and its appropriate evidence. There is too much at stake for you and the kingdom of God.

Then there is the Cross of Christ in our daily life "They that are Christ have crucified the flesh..." (Galatians 2:20) I am convinced that this experience happens when we are converted. But I also believe that there is a daily cross we are to bear. Jesus spoke of it in Matt 16:24," Then said Jesus unto his disciples, if any man will come after me, let him deny himself, and take up his cross, and follow me." I do not mean to imply that bearing the cross is an endurance contest. It is said of our Lord Jesus that he endured the cross because of the joy that was laid before him. When I asked Alma to be my wife I never thought for a second about what I was giving up. I was so glad to get her that what I gave up was not a sacrifice, but a privilege. If you and I are going to have real victory then we must bring our entire self under the weight of the cross. The Devil has a plan for your soul and he will use your body to accomplish his goal. Our only hope is the power of God working in our lives through the obedience to the word of God.

When the Psalms reveal the word of God as a lamp and a light he is showing us that the dark places in our journey can be illuminated. Part of our problem is we want to pick and choose only that part of the word of God that we are most comfortable with. Have you ever had a doctor prescribe some medications with the instructions to make sure you take all of the medicine? The doctor knows that the medication can only prevent you from a relapse if you take all of it and whatever is causing the difficulty has been destroyed.

Take the word of God into your system, take it on a daily basis. I know there are many leaders who suggest that you read the Bible through every year. I know from experience that reading the Bible like that there is very little, if any, of the bread of life digesting into your system. I would like to suggest that you read the Bible systematically, don't get in a hurry to get through like a racer stretching for the finishing line. In your reading stop and enjoy the journey, allow the word of God to speak to you. Don't worry whether you read, one chapter or forty, the idea is to absorb its contents. I suggest you keep a small spiral notebook and when a passage impacts you write it down and then give your thoughts about the passage. I find it helps to record the date. I even record the time of day.

Let me share with you a verse of Scripture found in Colossians 3: 16 that has impacted my life now for many years "Let the word of Christ dwell in you richly..." That little word "in" means at home, let the word of God be at home. Home is where I am most comfortable, it is where I want to be. Let the word of God find a home in your heart. There is another passage of Scripture that has meant a lot to me. It is Psalms 1:1-4 where there is listed four steps to prosperity and four reward.

First Get Good Advice

Verse one, "Blessed is the man who walks not in the counsel of the ungodly.

Do not get your advice from the ungodly, the world's system is not your measuring rod.

Second , Watch Your Interests.

Verse one, "Nor standeth in the way of sinners."

If you are going to have God's favor you must be interested in what affects God? God has a purpose in your live and it involves the reaching of lost humanity.

Third, Watch Your Motives.

Verse one, "Nor sitteth in the seat of the scornful"

When you sit with the scornful long enough it will affect your attitude; your attitude will affect your conduct. You don't have to put other people down to prosper in God's plan.

Forth, Feed in Good Stuff.

Verse two, "His delight is in the law of the Lord, and in his law doth he meditate day and night.

To delight in it is to relish in it. The term "law of the Lord "is a term used to describe the whole Word of God. "In his law he meditates day and night." The idea is to think on it absorb it, to apply it. Psalms 37:4 "Delight yourself also in the Lord and he shall give you the desires of your heart."

Notice the pay off for following the direction of God's word.

First, there will be stability in your life.

Verse three, "He shall be like the tree planted by the rivers of water"

Second, your life will be productive.

Verse three, "... Bring for fruit in its season"

This production will last well into old age. "They shall still bear fruit in old age; they shall be fresh and flourishing." (Psalms 92: 14)

Third, your influence will be lasting.

Verse three, "whose leaves do not wither"

Fourth, this is real prosperity.

Verse three, "and whatsoever he doeth shall prosper.

God blesses people who are working, people who are busy in the Lord's work whatever their responsibility is.

## Walking in the Spirit is Ever Listening for the Voice of the Spirit

I know from experience that the Spirit communicates to each of us differently. To live in the Spirit is to live conscious of his presence and guidance even when you don't feel it. The early Christians in selecting deacons were told by the apostles, "Seek out among you seven men of good reputation and full of the Holy Ghost and wisdom, whom we may appoint over this business." (Acts 6:3)

It is said of Barnabas that he was a good man and full of the Holy Ghost. (Acts 11: 24) This leads us to understand that being full of the Holy Ghost is a recognizable presence in one's life.

The Holy Spirit will communicate with us when we are entering a danger zone. In the early '60s I was pastoring in one of the northern states. I was very young; Alma and I had only been married for seven years. One afternoon I received a phone call from a young lady wanting me to come and pray for her. I never thought for a second that I was in any danger. So like a trusting pastor, I got in my car and was on my way when I heard a voice that sounded like it was coming from the back seat. The voice said, "You had better be careful!" The voice was so clear that I stopped the car and looked in the back seat. I suddenly realized that it was a Divine warning. I then had a word of knowledge. I knew she had laid a trap for me. God also gave me a word of wisdom. I knew exactly what to do about it. I followed the instructions and was saved from the enemy's attack. I shudder to think what might have happened if the Holy Spirit had not interfered on my journey that day. I would say most of the time there is no voice but only a strong feeling of being in danger. I believe this feeling comes from the Holy Spirit who is our constant guide. When this happens there will be an accompanying wisdom of what needs to be done.

Paul and Silas were planning on going to Asia, however; God had different plans for them. They felt the restraining hand of the Spirit forbidding them to go. There is no indication on how the Holy Spirit directed and guided Paul. To be guided by the Spirit we must be sensitive to his touch, he uses our intellect as well as our feelings to guide us.

I was in a mission service in Virginia, the sermon was completed and I was in the process of explaining the faith commitment cards when I had an unusual feeling of desperation that someone was in danger. I stopped what I was doing and opened my heart and mind to the Spirit. I explained to the people that God was doing something that I did not understand. Suddenly a man stood up in the back of the church, I never saw him until he stood up. I asked, "Are you the one God is dealing with?" He said yes and began to come forward. After a long time of praying the man was delivered and gave his heart to the Lord. We then learned that he had intended to cause trouble that night but God intervened and put him under arrest.

My wife is a gifted singer however she does more than just sing she ministers a song. Alma has related to me that sometimes when she is singing she will hear a name deep down in her spirit. When this happens she is drawn to a single person she then ministers to that person while she is singing. I have seen people delivered from depression as well as physical healing. There is such a world of difference when we stay open to the Spirit and allow him to have his way.

CHAPTER

# 12

# THE SPIRIT CONTROLLED CHURCH

It is possible to excel in mechanics and fail in dynamics. The real work of the church depends upon the power of the Holy Spirit. When we read the history of the early church you are struck with the fact that when a person was filled with the Spirit there was a difference in the effectiveness of their ministry. I tell you the truth that power is self-evident! Even demons know the difference.

The Holy Spirit is perceived as power and influence rather than a person. There is a sense in which we view the Spirit as water, we think of the Holy Spirit in terms of being filled with or to be submerged in the Holy Spirit. We think of him as something you feel with no ability to have a personal relationship. When we think of Him in this way we do Him an injustice. It is not power, the power is a person. You are filled and controlled by a person, the person of the Holy Spirit. Notice the apostolic benediction. "The communion of the Holy Ghost be with you all." (2 Cor.13: 14) Communion means a partnership. If you run references on this word you will find the idea of sharing runs through them all. The communion of the Holy Spirit therefore means that we are partners and colleagues with the Spirit of God.

The Spirit needs the church and the church needs the Spirit. Both are partners depending on each other to accomplish the work of the Lord. That is why the work of the Spirit is always linked to the life of the church. The power of the church is associated with the presence of the Spirit. The church derives its authority from the risen Christ and the Spirit then works through a praying and concentrated people. The church that has authority to bind and to loose is a church agreed in prayer and gathered in the name of the Lord Jesus.

The Spirit and the church cannot be independent of each other. The Holy Spirit must feel welcome and when he is welcome there is power to destroy the kingdom of darkness. The power is not in organization nor is it in wealth or learning. It is still true it is by my Spirit saith the Lord. (Zach.4: 6) Many churches seem to be frustrated by the lack of power that transforms lives. There is confusion about what it takes to build a successful church. I am not convinced that the big churches are the only ones that are successful. We have designed methods and programs that we feel will fulfill our greatest expectation but far too often the expectation is wasted. I believe part of the answer is in changing our objectives.

I have noticed over the years that people are attracted to a church where love is the rule, where people feel welcome and accepted not criticized. I was visiting a church some time ago that was complaining because their church was not growing. There were two things that stood out to me. First, there was such a critical spirit about what people did or did not do that people were afraid that they could not measure up to their expectations. Second, I heard them say many times, "We are a family." That sounds good but to me they were so close that it was difficult to break in and become a part of their family. Where love ruler, people feel welcome and accepted they are then able to work out there own salvation with fear and trembling. (Phil.2: 12)

What I mean by changing our objectives, let the focus be upon praise allowing the Holy Spirit to do his perfect work. Notice Jesus said, "when he is come he will..." (John 16: 8) Jesus was talking about the Holy Spirit and there is a work that only he can do! The Holy Spirit will do his work if he is not ignored. Sometimes we can become so impressed with our own program that we are not aware that we have been ignoring the Holy Spirit. I like a good musical program, it adds balance and prepares the people to hear the word of God. We can spend hours rehearsing the music to make sure we get it right let us not forget to season it with prayer. I believe in the preached word however, I know from experience that it is possible to get so involved in the sermon that we never realize that the Spirit had already closed the message a long time before we got through.

Gordon Fee book, God's Empowering Presence, quoted in Christianity Today, Jan. 17, 1996 The title of the article was, "Have we domesticated the Holy Spirit." Fee speaks of the church when he says, "We have tamed the Holy Spirit and in the process rendered our witness ineffective." He goes on to say, "Paul's understanding of the role of the Holy Spirit in the local church and the way the church operates today don't match up." Fee says, "The key element of spirituality that is lacking in the contemporary church is the realization that heaven (not as a place but as a promise time) has come to earth in the presence of the Spirit. Because of this Spirit invasion the church should be living out the heavenly life in the here and now." I find Fee's comments fascinating that a part of heaven has come down to earth in the person of the Holy Spirit. It is not that we believe in the possibility of miracles but we believe in the absolute necessity of them in the life of a New Testament church.

F.J. May in his book, Acts and Church Growth, enumerates all of the places where the gifts of the Spirit contributed to the growth of the young church. It is impossible to count the many miracles that appeared in the early church. "And by the hand of the apostles were many signs and wonders wrought among the people." (Acts 5:12) Even when Peter was walking down the street people would move there sick so that the shadow of Peter would fall across them. (Acts 5:15) They were special miracles wrought by Paul in that pieces of cloth that were touched by the man of God brought healing to people. (Acts 19:11-12) It may be impossible to prove that every miracle provided an opportunity for evangelism. It does seem to be indicated in Mark's Gospel, chapter 16, where spreading the gospel of Jesus is directly connected to signs following. In Matthew 16: 18 Jesus makes a direct promise" I will build my church." The authority to do this is in verse 19 "and I will give unto you the keys of the kingdom of heaven and whatsoever thou shall bind on earth shall be bound in heaven and whatsoever thou shall loose on earth shall be loosed in heaven."

Jesus had just asked the disciples about what the people were saying about him. (Matt 16:13) Their answer proves they did not know who he was. Then Jesus put the question directly to them. Peter's confession was calm and calculated from the experience God unfolded to him. "Thou art the Christ the son of the living God."(V 16) Jesus said, based on this confession of Peter, "I will build my church and the gates of hell will not prevail against it." Then Jesus said, "I give unto you the keys of the kingdom of God." There are those who feel this set of keys were given to Peter making him the leader. However, the disciples did not understand Jesus' words to mean that Peter and his successors held the keys to the kingdom. Keys speak of authority keys, opened doors that are otherwise closed.

The church in Philadelphia is one of only two out of seven that is not told to repent. The resurrected Lord said to this faithful church... "He that is true, he that has the key of David, he that opens and no man shutteth, and shutteth, and no man openeth." (Rev.3: 7) The Lord is pictured here as having the keys of authority to open and close doors, as he deems necessary. In verse eight he gives the church a golden opportunity, "I know thy works, behold I have set before you an open door."

When you look at the whole body of truth you come to understand that there are doors that only the omnipotent one can open. The keys that are given in Matthew 16 can only be used when the Lord sets before us an open door.

In Acts 16: 6, "now when they had gone throughout Phrygia and the regions of Galatia, and were forbidden of the Holy Ghost to preach the word in Asia." Then again in verse 7, "After they were come to Mysia, they assayed to go into Bithynia but the Spirit suffered them not to go." It is evident that Asia, which today is Turkey, was not ready for the gospel. The Lord did not open the door for Paul and Silas to use the keys of the kingdom.

## Second, the Binding and Loosening.

Notice the binding and loosening is a result of using the keys of the kingdom. In rabbinical language to loose is to permit and to bind is to forbid. This is spiritual authority that comes to those who give themselves to the work of the kingdom through prayer and the proclamation of the gospel.

It is evident that many of us have fallen far short of Paul's method of evangelism. It seems to me that the easiest thing we do is to preach, and that is very important,however, we need the performance of the message. I believe the reason this has happened is some preachers who have become very popular have such a weird and whack theology that we don't want to be associated with them. I remember in the early '50s, as a teenager, I attended a healing crusade. The evangelist was well known and a very popular in the healing ministry. There were a number of people who claimed to be healed that I had no way of knowing if it were true or not. But then there was a boy no more than five or six years old who had one leg two inches shorter than the other. I watched as the evangelist took off the boy,s shoe and placed him on a table so all could see. I watched as the evangelist prayed for the boy and his leg grew to be the same length as the other. Some 20 years later, the evangelist is now dead, and I was reading a book that told how he was so mixed up in his doctrine that the men who worked with him did their best to keep him from preaching because he always made people angry. I must admit to you there are some things that I do not understand and this is one of them. I believe it is cases like this that have caused some to back away from the ministry of deliverance and use this as and excuse to be only a token Pentecostal. I call all of us not to be afraid of allowing the Holy Spirit to work his complete will with gifts and manifestations.

When we gather to worship and the Holy Spirit is welcome, there is a sense of awe that God is among us. A sense of complete unworthiness balanced by a feeling of total joy because of his grace. We must never forget that the Holy Spirit is not just a force or an influence but a person who reveals himself through believers. God intended for the church, who is made up of individuals, to operate through the gifts of the Spirit; it is in this way the church receives edification. The fruit of the Spirit gives balance to the gifts of the Spirit. In the fruit of the Spirit there is a concern for one another and absence of a take over spirit. When the fruit of the Spirit is dominant there is not only individual piety but also corporate holiness.

CHAPTER

# 13

# THE CHURCH'S GREATEST CHALLENGE

A denomination can quickly become a dinosaur that is unable to adapt to the needs of humanity. The local church, in some cases, is only interested in those needs that have a return interest to them; convalescent homes, senior citizens, world missions and the little people are expendable because of an improper understanding of the purpose of the local church. If we are not careful we will be pulling apart and treating one another as distant cousins rather than members of the same family.

It would be interesting if all of us would respond to the following question. "What is the purpose of the local church?" It would be a very interesting response especially if every one would be totally honest.

I can well imagine that those pastors in the middle of a building program would feel that the top priority was to get their building finished before they go crazy. Others may have a similar response as they view their own problems and difficulties of doing the Lord's work. But I want us to go beyond the daily grind of just getting through another week. I want us to look through Calvary's sacrifice, past the empty to tomb to the present-day, and ask the Lord to help us as a church to fulfill God's ultimate purpose in the here and now. I will, by the help of the good Lord, bring some of them to your mind for your consideration.

## The First Challenge Is to Be Like Christ in an Ungodly World.

Acts 11:26, "...and the disciples were called Christian first Antioch." Barnabas was sent by the apostles to check out what was happening at Antioch. It didn't take Barnabas long to realize he needed some help. Barnabas when to Tarsus to get Saul to assist him in this new work. These two giants of the faith taught the people for one year and had great success. The people of the city of Antioch, Mr. "ordinary" citizen, gave them the name "Christian." It was bestowed on them because of what the people saw in their lives. There is a tremendous contrast between light and darkness and there was a tremendous contrast between the men of Antioch and the followers of Christ. Antioch was the third largest city in the Roman Empire, out ranked only by Rome and Alexandria. It was the capitol of the Roman Province of Syria and was known as the Queen of the East. Their morals were very corrupt. They had ritual prostitution in the temple of Daphne. Antioch was a great pleasure resort and it gained and evil reputation for immorality. I am sure as the new believers accepted Christ; their lives went under a radical transformation. This change was so radical that it seemed as a rebuke to the average citizen of Antioch. You see a genuine Christian who follows Christ takes on in his conduct the nature of Christ. What a refreshing experience it is to meet a person whom it becomes evident that Christ lives through them.

In this day we have been taught all the techniques of living successfully and being happy. I say we have been taught them, that is a misnomer. It is pumped at us all day in multiplied thousands of commercials that happiness depends on a positive attitude and keeping your body in good physical condition. Yet it is ironic that we have endeavored to take the labor out of work and so we have gotten further and more out of shape. This has spawned a whole industry of physical fitness craze. It appears we have not learned anything at all. We are bored in spite of the fact we have so much to entertain us.

Have we lost, as a church, the meaning of the cross in our daily lives? Paul says "but God forbid that I should glory, save in the cross of our Lord Jesus Christ by whom the world is crucified unto me, and I unto the world" (Galatians 6:14) Paul says, "I am crucified onto the world." Paul means that there are things about this present evil world that will destroy you. The only sure cure for victory is to take this earthly body to the cross and die there. It is only then that Christ can live through you.

Strange as it may seem there are some who hear these messeges that will throw up their hands and declare it to be impossible. But I challenge you to find a new convert, who has just been set free from his burden of sin and he will came closer to embracing what I'm saying than some Christians of long-standing whose theology has been polluted by too much "menology". These Christians are more interested in pleasing the individual than pleasing the Lord. Some sermons I hear are suited more for the psychology book than the book of Acts. There is no evidence that the name "Christian" was given them in duration and mockery. It was a means of identification. The Disciples referred to themselves as followers of the way, as believers and brothers in Christ. I believe their lives match their sermons and testimonies. It seemed natural to call them after the man they followed and emulated. Paul put his finger on the problem we are facing today; the world is trying to squeeze us into its mold. (Romans 12:2)

A Christian is a combination of Christ and you. They talk of Christ, live for Christ, and work for Christ. They had caught his Spirit! They were occupied with his business, they were manifested him in character and conduct; and the men of Antioch said these men are Christians. There is a secret of living the Christ life that is devoid of struggle and frustration and is as natural as breathing. Paul says the reason is "Christ in you the hope of glory" (Colossians 1:27) It is his living presence within us that constrains us to loyalty and creates compassion in us for others. We are facing a hostile and cynical world. They have seen the carpet baggars who have claimed so much but have demonstrated by their actions that their ultimate loyalty was to their own comfort and prestige. The world will not listen to our message unless our life goes before our message.

If we are going to be like Christ we must take his instruction on attitude and conduct. Here are two truths that I feel are very important. **First**, Jesus said if you are to obtain mercy you must show mercy. (Matthew 5:7) We have plenty of laws but have showed very little mercy. There have been many times in my life when I wanted to show mercy but I did not want to be perceived as being soft on sin. Check the way Jesus treated the woman caught in the act of adultery. Notice his words, "Neither do I condemn you, go and sin no more." Mercy and grace come from the same eternal fountain of God's love. Mercy is the ability of God to withhold punishment we rightfully deserve until grace arrives. You could say grace travels on the road that mercy builds mercy does not eliminate the need of discipline. Mercy is on attitude.

**Then look at something else** Jesus said, the only people who will be called the children of God are the peacemakers

(Matthew 5: 9) A peacemaker is one who lays aside his own interest for the peaceful good of the whole. God will be the judge of some of our churches that appear more like battle stations that a peaceful oasis. As long as we make our decisions based on what people will think about us we will never make the right decisions. This is why Jesus was called a winebibber and a friend of sinners.

In a number of our large cities, in the summertime, some gifted young people go to a run down part of the city and set up a puppet stage. The music and all the pictures speak of cartoon characters that draw the kids to their puppet show. There is no mention of Jesus until the last part of the show. Then a little puppet that has been the hero comes on stage. He begins to relate the character of Jesus without calling his name, "I know a man who has tender hands, they never touch you except in love." He goes on to say his eyes show such compassion. The whole time he is describing Jesus without mentioning his name when a little boy in the back of the other kids began to jump up-and-down, "I know who you are talking about! Old Joe he lives on my street." That little boy recognized in Old Joe the character Jesus.

In a very old book, "Plutarch's lives," Alexander the Great had conquered a certain city.The leading family of that city, with all of their jewels, gold and silver were brought before him to render a judgment as to whether they should live or die. There sat Alexander with his coat of gold and before him stood a young man, his beautiful wife and his wife's mother. Alexander looked at the young man and said, "What would you do for your life?" The man said, "I would give you all my gold, all my silver, all the properties for my life." And Alexander looked at him a bit and said, "What would you give for the life of this beautiful young wife of yours?" The young man stepped out and said, "I would give my life, sir." Alexander with the great power, which was his, waved his hand and said, "Go free." He got up from the judgment seat and walked out. As he walked out the mother turned to the daughter and said, "Daughter, did you notice that beautiful gold coat that Alexander wore?" And the daughter said, "No mother, I had eyes only for him who said, as for me I would give my life for her."

Oh how I love Jesus. I have loved him in life; I shall love him in death. When I shall see him in the glory, I am going to say with a tongue of eloquence that is not possible in this tenement of clay, "I love you, Jesus, because you first loved me.

## The Second Challenge is Reproduction in an Ungodly World. In Acts 26:28 "almost thou persuadest me to be a Christian"

Two men fill this scene. The one is dressed in the royal robe and color of a King. The other man is dressed in prison clothes and for his accessories, a heavy chain. Paul is defending himself against charges brought by the Jews who wanted him destroyed.

The Hall of Audience was where the trial was held. It was a large room long and narrow. They were two doors one at the far end of the room where dignitaries and special guests made their entrance. The other door was on the side, a little beyond halfway, where the common guests and prisoners were allowed to enter to attend whatever function they were having. The room was decorated in bright colors of royalty. A large chandelier hung in the center of the room suspended by a chain. The chain allowed it to be lowered so servants could light the oil lamps. Then smaller lamps were placed along the walls to give extra light to the room.

King Agrippa and his sister Bernice were here to pay their respects to the new governor Festus. Agrippa was a regional King appointed by Caesar and reign at Caesar's pleasure. Paul had been a thorn in the side of the Jewish leaders for many years; they were proud of him in his early years before the Damascus road experience. Paul, who then was known as Saul, had demonstrated great enthusiasm for persecution and destroying all that claimed to be followers of a man that had been crucified, whom they claimed was raised from the dead. But one day in the hollowed halls of Herod's temple in Jerusalem, the word was spreading that young Saul had lost his senses. The rumors were that he claimed to have seen Jesus in a vision, and since then no one has seen him.

Now, they knew the whole story. They had heard it many times. These self-righteous Jewish leaders hated Paul almost as much as they hated Jesus. They had laid a trap for him between Jerusalem and Caesarea where they were taking him to be heard by the authorities in Caesarea. Paul's nephew had heard their plans and reported it to the chief captain. Paul was rushed early to Caesarea under heavy guard. The Jewish leaders tried to get Paul transferred to Jerusalem where they would have a better chance of success, but they were denied.

Festus had asked Agrippa to hear Paul and help him identify the charges that would accompany him to Rome. Paul had for a long time felt the desire to preach the gospel in Rome; he felt this was God's plan. Paul had exercised his right as a Roman citizen to appeal to Caesar.

The room was full; some came out of duty while others came out of curiosity. The scene is set; two men represent two different worlds. One man representing a history of murder maneuvers for power, incest, and moral decay. The other man Paul, God's preacher man, representing the resurrected Lord and Savior, and a lifestyle of holy living.

The King gave the orders to bring in the prisoner. There is excitement in the room and a hush came over the crowd. You could hear the rattling of chains coming down the hall and then - there he is- Paul with chains dangling about his stooped physical unimposing stature. There is more to this man than what appears. He is the New Testament Daniel in a lion's den and the lions had better be careful. I believe that when Paul entered the room he paused a minute to look over the crowd. I believe the only one he recognized was his old traveling buddy, Aristarchus. Paul referred to Aristarchus as my fellow prisoner. (Colossians 4:10) He identified with Paul at Ephesus and was with him through all of his imprisonment. He was a prisoner by choice. He made Paul's life his life because he had a sensitive heart. There are people who can't lead a service and they may not have great talent but they are helpers. They are burden bearers and we need them and God needs them.

Agrippa speaks, "Paul you are permitted to speak for yourself." Listen as Paul makes a brilliant introduction. "I feel very happy to answer for myself," he says with a gesture of his hand "I know you are an expert in the customs of the Jews." Paul plows into his defense. He is clear and direct, no beating around the bush for Paul. He looks straight at the King. "I am judged of the promise made of God onto our fathers. For this sake, King Agrippa, I am accused of the Jews. Paul clearly identifies this hope as the resurrection. From verse nine through eighteen Paul presents his testimony. It began with him persecuting the Jesus people his relentless obsession to destroy all who followed Jesus. The Damascus road experience, where he met Jesus-Paul cried out, "Who are thou, Lord?" The voice of Jesus was clear as the breaking of a new day. "I am Jesus whom thou persecutest" Paul is instructed as to the reason for this divine intervention from heaven. It is not all good there will be a lifetime of suffering. The late C.M.Ward says, "Paul saw the inside of ever respectable jailed from Jerusalem to Rome." Throughout Paul's life there were very few quiet nights. Everywhere he went there was either a revival or a riot. The focus changes and Paul began to draw the net around the King. I am sure that Felix the ex-governor told Festus, the new governor, how Paul had pressed him about righteousness, temperance and judgment to come. It affected Felix so strongly that he trembled. There is reason to believe that Festus probably said to Felix, "watch out for this prisoner he is a Jesus nut."

Festus shouted, Paul "you're crazy!" He may have said you read to many books, spend too much time staring off into space. Paul refused to be deterred. He had a big fish on the line and he was not about to let him go. Paul says, "The King knows these things they were not done in a corner."

"King Agrippa beliveth thou the prophets? I know that you believe!" Then Agrippa said unto Paul, "Almost thou persuadeth me to be a Christian." There is no doubt Agrippa feels the weight of Paul's eternal words. However, there is a note of sarcasm in Agrippa's response to Paul. G. Campbell Morgan says that the real meaning of Agrippa's words have been misused over the years. What he is actually saying is, "with but little persuasion thou would vain make me a Christian." (The Life of Christian – Morgan, Page 17)

Paul still in chains says "that what I am praying for whether now or later and not only you but everyone listening today, to become like me except of course this prison jewelry." (Peterson, The Message Acts 26:29)

There is such a strong distaste for evangelism it is often viewed by those who are outside the Church, as though I am right and you're wrong and I'm going to change you to be like me. There may be such zeal to win people that we pressure them for a decision before the Holy Spirit has time to do his work. One may persuade in such a convincing manner that he wins the day, but loses for eternity. The work of convincing them of their need to change and let Christ into their heart is not our work but the work of the Holy Spirit. "When he is come, he will reprove the world of righteousness temperance and judgment" (John 16:8) We are to present the message in a loving way surrounded with prayer and then let the Holy Spirit do his work. Victory to the preacher is not always measured in the number of conversions but in the truth and clarity of the message.

## Third the Challenge of Suffering in an Ungodly World.

1 Peter 4:16 "Yet if any man suffer as a Christian, let him not be ashamed; let him glorify God on this behalf."

There is something that needs to be said about the value of suffering. However, before we get to that we will need to look at verse 15 of the same chapter "...let none of you suffer as a murderer, or as a thief, or as an evildoer, or as a busybody in other men's matters."

The first thing Peter says, *don't suffer as a murderer.* It appears that Peter is writing to a group of Christians suffering for their faith. It seems out of place for him to say be careful that you don't suffer as a murderer. A murderer is one who takes someone else's life. It is always sad when you read about someone taking another's life. However, there is more than one way to take a life 1John 3:15, "Whosoever hated his brother is a murderer: and ye know that no murderer has eternal life abiding in him." He said in verse 14 that the way the world knows you have passed from death to life is if you love the brethren. When he speaks here of love, it is singular, but when he speaks in hate it is plural. How does this hate display itself? It is displays by the way we are willing to believe any rumors that circulate especially if it is negative. Evil and malicious gossip that assassinates a person's character is murder. Deuteronomy 27:24 pronounced a curse on the person who smite his neighbor secretly. If you have ever had someone whom you trusted misrepresent something you have said or just told a boldface lie if you have had to suffer through the stinging arrows of accusation that is always just beyond your grasp; then you know what it means to murder someone. But known assuredly that the one who participates in this kind of illegal act will not go unpunished. If you are a Christian, don't get caught participating in such a murderous act of character assassination.

## Don't Suffer as a Thief

A thief is someone who has taken what does not belong to him; to obtain by whatever means available something that belongs to someone else. A person is a thief because he does not have an adequate appreciation for what belongs to someone else. There are those who would not rob a bank or take twenty dollars from the cash drawer but will in different ways take advantage of the opportunity to take little items that seem so frivolous.

A young lady asked me if it was wrong to take a box of Kleenex from the motel room after spending the night. The fact that she asked said she had doubts about whether it was right. If there is a question, then comes down on the side of caution. I believe that stealing has become an excitable way of doing business for most companies. They just write it off as a loss.

When Alma and I were first married I worked for the Buick Motor Division. I worked on a cutting machine that trims off the rough edges of a part that housed the transmission. The quota for that machine was set and I was responsible to run that many during my shift. I was informed that they ran the counter up by hand, giving a false reading on how many parts that had been run. I was new and it was my first day when the men informed me of their practice. I refused, it did not make me very popular with the boys but to me it was stealing.

## Don't Suffer as a Busybody in Other Men's Matters.

This is a person whose busies himself with what does not concern him, pries into affairs of another, one who attempts to control or direct them as if they were his own. Solomon says "it is an honor for a man to cease from strife; but every fool will be meddling (Proverbs 20:3) Paul in writing to the church at Thessalonica, "We hear that there are some which walk among you disorderly. Working not all, but are busybody. (11 Thessalonians 3:11) Again in Proverbs 26: 20, "Where there is no talebearer, the strife ceaseth."

Look at verse 16. "Yet if anyone suffer as a Christian let him not be ashamed but let him glorify God in this behalf." The NIV translates that last line as, "... But praise God that you bear the name."

Listen to some Scriptures on suffering.1 Peter 2:20-22, "For it is commendable if a man bear up under pain of unjust suffering because he is conscious of God. But how is it to your credit if you receive a beating for doing wrong and endure it? To this you were called because Christ suffered for you, leaving you an example that you should follow in his steps. But if you suffer for doing good and you endure it, that is commendable before God." By reading these verses you get the feeling that suffering for your faith is something that cannot be avoided. We learn obedience from suffering in Hebrews 5:8, "though he was a son yet learned he obedience by the things he suffered." Whatever be the depth of meaning of this verse, as it applies to Christ, when we look at it and apply it to ourselves, we are made to realize that God uses many different experiences, some negative and some positive, to teach us obedience. How many times has God allowed us to get flat on our back so that he could talk to us? I have no doubt that the enemy of our soul plans and executes attacks against us but God intervenes and we are able to not only rise to victory, but learned one of Satan's ultimate tricks.

We learn stability through suffering. The song that says if you never have a problem you would not know God could solve them. Look at 1 Peter 5:8 RSV-be self-controlled and alert- the King James says- be sober, be vigilant, your enemy the devil prowls around like a roaring lion looking for someone to devour. It may be elementary to say that this verse teaches me that the devil is my enemy and that's very important to know. This verse also teaches me that the devil growls a lot, he makes a lot of noise and that is only a scare tactic. But the most important thing I learned from this verse is the devil is seeking someone to devour which means he cannot devour just anybody he pleases. In James 4:7, "Submit yourself therefore to God. Resist the devil, and he will flee from you." I am still on my subject, I have said all this to give you a backdrop for the next verse of 1 Peter 4:10, "And the God of all grace, who calls you to his eternal glory in Christ, after you have suffered a little while, will himself restore you and make you strong, firm and steadfast." Strong means strength to endure, not flabby: the foundation is solid, steadfast in the faith.

Paul gives glory to God for his life testimony. It is summed up in Philippians 3:8, "Yea doubtless, and I count all things but loss for the excellence of the knowledge of Christ Jesus my Lord: for whom I have suffered the loss of all things, and do count them but dung that I might win Christ."

I know that some people believe if you have enough faith you can avoid suffering of all kinds. It sounds so good but it is so full of holes it will never float. No one has a greater faith and power than Paul. Yet with all the miracles of healing that God honored his work with and the special miracles recorded in Acts, he could not avoid the beating he suffered or the jail he slept in or the ax that separated his head from his body. I believe the devil is waging a war of intimidation. The carnal man reasons, don't rock the boat just get along, God knows how you feel and he will understand. This is such a subtle approach to appeal to our need of self-preservation.

As a Christian who has been delivered from this present evil world, there has entered into our live a devotion to Christ not a historical Christ, but to a living Christ. I'm not talking about emulating Christ. The fact that is establishing in eternity Christ, himself, the living present, eternal Christ has taken possession of the inner man and from that center, directs, controls, suggests, and in this way reveals himself through our lives. A Christian is a revelation of Christ. We are living in this world but we measure everything by the standard of eternity. No one can live like that without suffering a reproach. If Christ lives in you he cannot be hid. It is impossible to hide his light, it will shine through.

Nicodemus and Joseph Arimathea may have been secret disciples, but when the crisis came and all the rest ran away they begged the master's body and bore it tenderly to the burial. So in conclusion when the suffering comes, bear his name well, do not be ashamed. But glorify God in the name you bear. **You are a Christian!**